Rewire Your Brain

Learn How to Switch On Your Brain, Unf*ck Yourself and Heal Your Body by Eliminating Anxiety and Phobias. Discover the Key to Peak Happiness and System Thinking

By James T. Covey

© **Copyright 2020 - All rights reserved.**

The content contained within this book may not be reproduced, duplicated or transmitted without direct written permission from the author or the publisher.

Under no circumstances will any blame or legal responsibility be held against the publisher, or author, for any damages, reparation, or monetary loss due to the information contained within this book. Either directly or indirectly.

Legal Notice:

This book is copyright protected. This book is only for personal use. You cannot amend, distribute, sell, use, quote or paraphrase any part, or the content within this book, without the consent of the author or publisher.

Disclaimer Notice: Please note the information contained within this document is for educational and entertainment purposes only. All effort has been executed to present accurate, up to date, and reliable, complete information. No warranties of any kind are declared or implied. Readers acknowledge that the author is not engaging in the rendering of legal, financial, medical or professional advice. The content within this book has been derived from various sources. Please consult a licensed professional before attempting any techniques outlined in this book.

By reading this document, the reader agrees that under no circumstances is the author responsible for any losses, direct or indirect, which are incurred as a result of the use of information contained within this document, including, but not limited to, — errors, omissions, or inaccuracies.

Table of Contents

INTRODUCTION 5

CHAPTER 1: UNLEASH YOUR POTENTIAL 7

CHAPTER 2: HOW MINIMALISM CAN DRASTICALLY IMPROVE YOUR PRODUCTIVITY 13

CHAPTER 3: THE POWER OF FEELINGS AND THOUGHTS 22

CHAPTER 4: YOU ARE YOUR HABITS 47

CHAPTER 5: SILENCING YOUR MIND AND BEING PRESENT . 60

CHAPTER 6: WHAT GOOGLE DOESN'T TELL YOU ABOUT MEMORY 74

CHAPTER 7: ALL YOU NEED IS SELF-DISCIPLINE 81

CHAPTER 8: DECLUTTER YOUR BODY, MIND, TIME AND ENVIRONMENT 92

CHAPTER 9: HOW TO HIJACK YOUR CIRCUMSTANCES 104

CONCLUSION 116

Introduction

You might think that our brains can only change during childhood and adolescence, but they actually rewire themselves throughout our whole lives, including through our middle age and beyond.

It's never too late to learn a new skill and give your brain a workout. Stop making excuses for neglecting the most important muscle in your body. It craves learning and challenge. Give your brain what it wants.

The following chapters will discuss how the structure of your brain constantly changes. Every time you learn something new, the connections between your neurons rearrange. These connections are called synapses.

Synapses are the building blocks of your mind; this is good news for you because synapses change all the time. Anything is possible when you come to understand this.

When you study knowledge or practice skills, again and again, you reinforce your synapses, and they become stronger. The more you reinforce them through rehearsal, the stronger they get.

On the other hand, if you go a long time without reinforcing one of your synapses, it will eventually fade away. This is why our unused memories disappear after a while; this is called pruning.

The opposite of pruning is when you reinforce a synapse, firing your synapse. Understanding firing and pruning is essential to mastering the learning strategies in this book.

If you optimize these connections and declutter your mind, you will increase your productivity and unleash your unlimited memory power. In this book, you will learn how you can mold your brain into whatever you need it to be.

All it takes is using special learning strategies. These new techniques will make you think about your mind in ways you never have before.

There are plenty of books on this subject on the market, thanks again for choosing this one! Every effort was made to ensure it is full of as much useful information as possible, please enjoy!

Chapter 1: Unleash Your Potential

Live for Your Talent

All of us are on this planet for a reason. What have people always told you are good at? It feels awesome to be good at something. When you croon for your friends on karaoke night, fix your friend's refrigerator, or publish the mobile app you programmed, you remember that you have something to offer that no one else has.

I don't know what your special talent is, but everyone has one. If you didn't, you wouldn't be here right now.

If it isn't already, your talent needs to become one of the centers of your life. You have to spend a lot of time doing what you're good at if you want to feel good about your life. If you don't, everything starts to feel dull very quickly.

Every night before bed, think of this talent and think of how you will use it the next day. If you don't already have plans to use it, make plans. If work gets in the way, you need to reassess your priorities.

Life is too short to let your time be dictated by work. There's probably no reason to quit your job but think about your job as just one part of your life, not your whole life. You can't let it absorb all of your time.

If you have a family to take care of, remember that you don't have to choose between your family and your goals. Even if you spend fifteen minutes on your goals every day, you will feel better about your life.

Again, consistency is more important than quantity. If you stick with it and make reaching your goals part of your everyday routine, you make it a habit. You make it part of your life, part of your brain, part of you.

We have spent a little bit of time discussing the distinction between the conscious and unconscious brain, but now I want you to think about this a little bit more. It should seem a little bit strange if you think about what this really means. If there are parts of your brain that you aren't in control of, then who is in control of them?

The power of repetitive thought will help you see what I mean. At the same time of day that you work on the list that helps you with your goals, I want you to go over what is on this list mentally.

Think of it like reading out loud, but in your head. You can't let yourself just scan the words you wrote on the list like they are just part of an image. Words are sounds, and you would do well to learn that if you want to improve your brain. Vocalize the sounds on your list in your head. Do this every single day.

The next step is to start vocalizing the words on your list when you are not looking at the list. I don't know what kind of list you will have, so let me give you an example of what it might look like. This is going to be a lengthy list, so it should inspire a lot of ideas about what you should put in your own notes.

-Read a book
-Spend thirty minutes coding
-Go to the gym twice this week
-Look at other job opportunities near me
-Make more lists that cover possibilities that I could be missing
-Update my budget to save more money for the future
-Check my credit score and make my budget address the state of my credit
-Check my bank account once a day so I stay aware of how much money I have
-Spend some time meditating each day, even if it's only 15 minutes each day.
-Not necessarily while meditating, take a little bit of time to think about the larger universe. Think outside myself.
-Think about what I do every day, and how I could change that routine to make my future better.
-What did I do today that went above and beyond? Did I only do what was required of me because of work and family obligations?

-What am I doing tomorrow? What did I do yesterday?

-Am I eating well? Am I drinking enough water? Am I getting enough sleep? Am I smoking or drinking?

-Don't forget about the part of mindfulness that isn't meditation. Become more aware of the truth of my experience, much like when I notice the thoughts come to my mind while I focus on my breath.

-Let myself spend some length of time relaxing, but keep it to a limit. Don't let this repose go on and on without interruption. Because of the principle of inertia, I will let myself stay lazy unless I change my habit of being lazy. I will have to become the force that pushes me away from the direction of laziness.

Your list might end up looking a lot like this one, or it might barely look it like at all. But what matters is that you follow the two steps I gave you. First, practice reading out the sounds of the words of your list. Second, say the words on your list when you are not looking at it.

It might seem like a lot to memorize, but the more time you go over it, the easier it will become to learn. Think of it this way: if you were locked in a room and a speaker system kept repeating the Gettysburg Address, you would eventually learn this speech word for word. And it wouldn't even take that long. It also helps that your list will be an actual list of the goals of your life. It will be important to you; you care about the items on your list.

You don't have to memorize it word for word, either. As long as you can go over each item on your list without looking at it, you have it down.

Once you have it memorized, this list will become a big part of your life. It will be hard to stop going over it, because the things on the list really matter to you, and you want to do them. If you don't want to feel like you are neglecting the list, the solution is simple. Just live your life so that you are addressing your list every day.

There is one danger of using this strategy, though, so keep it in mind: if you aren't careful, going over the list will make you feel like you are actually doing something. If you repeat your list every day and it includes the item, "go to the gym twice a week," you need to actually go to the gym twice a week. You can't let yourself fall into the pattern of thinking that as long as it's on your memorized list, you will get to it when you need to. It is never convenient to start new behavior patterns. I have told you why many times now — your synapses are already arranged in a certain way, so any new ideas or behaviors will challenge your current system.

You need to use your imagination to see how your life would be different if you followed the items on your list. I am talking about deeply imagining what your life would really be like if you lived according to the changes.

When I was a kid, my little brother once said something that moved me. We watched a Superman movie, and he told me, "Wow, I wish I could fly!"

"I wish I could fly, too. It would be awesome."

"No, I mean, I wish I could really fly."

This moved me because it is one think to imagine something, but there are different levels of imagination. We can imagine that we could possibly fulfill our potential if we follow through with the items on our list. But we could also go further than that.

We could imagine that we really did what we said we would do on our list. No, I mean, really do them. There is nothing physically impossible that prevents this from happening. That means you are solely responsible. You have a list memorized; you know exactly what you need to do. Now is the time to simply stop pushing your goals to next month and do what you say you are going to do.

That list is now part of your unconscious brain, and parts of it will occur to you when you don't even intend it. You will be glad of this in the future. These thoughts will serve as a reminder that you have the potential. You had the potential to commit to memorizing a list of your goals. You have the potential to achieve them, too.

Chapter 2: How Minimalism Can Drastically Improve Your Productivity

Living Minimally in a Maximized World

The expectations people have of themselves today are monstrous. We are supposed to be smart, authentic, beautiful, healthy, professional, social, fun, witty, conscientious, and the list goes on.

Being all of these things at once is impossible. We humans only have a few basic needs. On the side of physical wellness, we need food, water, rest, and shelter.

Since humans are a little more complex than other animals, we also have a social need and a need for self-efficacy, which just means we need to have some control over our environment. Neglecting our physical needs will kill our bodies, but neglecting our human needs will kill our spirit.

If you want to optimize your brain and yourself, you have to become a minimalist. Otherwise, you will lose yourself in the cacophony of influences in our modern society.

Minimalism centers your body and spirit so you can focus on your dreams and take the small steps to achieve them. Every day go through this short list of needs and make sure you fulfill them. You don't need anything else.

You first need to evaluate how minimally you are living right now. Have many things do you own? How much do your utility bills add up to?

You don't have to judge yourself; as we've made abundantly clear, you are who you are today because of your past. You are who you are because of the synapses you have connected by this point. Everyone certainly needs to take a healthy amount of responsibility for their lives, but it would be foolish to say that you were able to control every tiny aspect of your life that made you who you are.

That means the usefulness of guilt is very low when you think about how minimally you are living. You might not be living minimally at all; maybe you do a lot of shopping and you distract yourself with a lot of electronic entertainment. There is a need for you to be honest with yourself about how those things affect you and how they hold you back but feeling guilty about it won't help you at all.

This is a good place to talk about emotions in the context of changing your lifestyle to be more minimal. You want to improve your brain and be smarter. You can understand how living more like a minimalist would help you get there. The challenges you will face won't make it easy, but you are determined to be better than you were before, so you won't let it stop you. However, you think of your past and feel like you wasted your great mind by living the way you have lived so far.

But this isn't the case at all. There is never a need for you to feel guilty about how you have already lived, because how you lived made you who you were. You weren't as wise about how your actions affect your brain as you are now, but you still are brilliant in many areas because of the ways you chose to spend your time.

These are the things that make you who you are; they make you unique. You should feel proud, not guilty.

It is true that you know better than you did before, so you want to make big changes. But look at your past as the "ground zero" for where you are now. You could call it your backstory like you are a fictional character, or you could say that you are a new person now.

You were a different person back then. Because of the elastic nature of the brain, we are constantly changing. There was definitely continuity between then and who you are now, but much more changed than stayed the same.

Your brain is never as comfortable with dramatic change as it is with continuity, but it changes nonetheless. It doesn't have a choice because we always have to adapt to new situations. You should think about what you have had to adapt to in your past. Think about how it changed you.

Before we begin talking about steps you need to take to become a minimalist, go back to the chapter about mindfulness meditation and meditate on how you had to change. If you need a refresher: try to focus only on the breath, and when you start thinking about something else, go back to the breath.

The main difference this time is you should go into the meditation thinking about the struggles you have gone through in your life. Think about how these struggles changed you, even though you didn't want to change.

In all reality, changing yourself to be a minimalist will be a lot easier than anything else you have gone through. You are not taking in a lot of new clutter to sort through. You are going to do the opposite. You will identify the clutter that is already in your life and you are going to get rid of it.

Once you have removed some of this clutter, your mind itself will feel less messy. They say that the state of one's room reveals the state of their mental condition, and almost nothing truer has ever been said. You might have a uniquely messy room, but even if that is true, taking the steps to clean it up is not as hard as you might think.

The first stage of living minimally is the part that most people think of. It is the most straightforward to get started, though it does take some amount of physical work. This stage requires that you appraise all the things that you own and ask yourself what your life would be like without them.

How many TV's do you need in your house? You surely don't need three or more. But do you even need two, one for your bedroom and one for your living room? I am about to say something you won't like, so be ready: do you really need a TV at all? You can't deny that it would make you smarter to watch TV less. If you aren't willing to admit that, you might not be ready to make the sacrifices that becoming more intelligent requires.

Living without a TV isn't essential to becoming a minimalist, but you should at least seriously consider it. It will help you think more like a minimalist. TVs are a great example of a thing that many people act like they can't live without, even though they absolutely could. We let ourselves believe that the way we have lived so far has to define the way we live the rest of our lives.

But improving your brain and living like a minimalist force you to rethink everything about how you have lived before. If you limit yourself to what you know, you can't make your brain smarter. It will stay stagnant. Not only are you not letting yourself imagine how things can be different, but you are keeping everything in your environment the same.

In the context of improving your brain, changing the environment around you is a fantastic way to let yourself think differently. In Chapter 5, we will go more over how the influences that surround you make you who you are. The people around you make you who you are because of mirror neurons. The objects that surround you make you who you are, too. They reflect on how you think about your life.

If you keep a messy room, that tells your brain that you are fine with sloppiness. It tells your brain that being surrounded by chaos is no problem.

You may have experienced this already: when you finally cleaned your room, you felt like a new person. Your mind felt clear, and it seemed like the possibilities were endless.

Being a minimalist is more work than cleaning your room, but not by much. Most of the work will be the emotional labor of letting go of items you are used to having around. And the positive impacts it will have on your brain will absolutely be worth it. Once you are through, you will wish you did this a long time ago.

The easier things to get rid of will be the things you have multiples of, like electronics or furniture. It might still be hard for you to let them go, but it isn't nearly as hard as getting rid of other things.

For those things, you don't want to work with a process of elimination. You want to work from a list of your favorite possessions. Not the things that you will get rid of, but the things that you truly can't imagine living without.

The best way to do this will practice our imagination once again. Imagine you are on a stranded island. There is not a set number of things you can have with you, but the island can't look like your home. You will have to make some sacrifices and leave some things behind.

When you are writing the list, don't walk around your home inspecting the things you want to bring to the island. Work from memory alone. If something hasn't left enough of an impression on you to conjure it from memory, you don't need it. It just takes up space; it doesn't make you happier.

Once you have this list written, forget about all the things you didn't write down. You didn't even imagine them on the island with you, so you really don't need them.

Your home will feel more like your own when you have fewer things in it. Each item that you have will serve a purpose other than just taking up space. You will actually have a use for each of them.

A "use" can mean a lot of things. An object having a use doesn't mean it has to be like a toothbrush and directly make a task possible. Even a small piece of decoration can have an important use. In this case, you can think of beauty as a practical use. You want to feel happy and comfortable in your own home, so beauty has a lot of use here.

The other way around works too, though. Just because you can use an object for something does not mean that you have to keep it. If you have a use for something, but only once a year or less, give it away. You don't really need it. If you do need it, you can borrow it from someone else. You can buy it later down the road if it actually turns out to be necessary.

But the problem is that people often lie to themselves about what they need. They say that they truly need something, but when they close their eyes and imagine all the things that go to the stranded island with them, that thing doesn't even come with them.

It's possible that you have noticed how minimalism can be a metaphor for brain improvement. Minimalism relates to many of the big ideas in this book. Becoming a minimalist is to declutter the physical things in your home as becoming a mastermind is to decluttering the physical things in your brain.

They are highly connected. Your home is a reflection of who you are on the inside, so you should take care of it. Taking care of it requires that you don't leave things in there that have no use.

A big gap between people who succeed in minimalism and people who don't is pure willingness. If you really wanted to clear your home of distractions that ultimately keep you from reaching your true potential, you would do it.

From what we have learned so far, it should be clear to you why minimalism would be a necessary step in being the person you want to be. It's possible that you won't be willing to go through with it, though. Your life is yours to live, so you can live with your own choices. If you believe that you really need that grandfather clock, keep it.

But one day you will hopefully come to realize that growth requires sacrifice. You won't be able to improve your brain if you keep everything in your life the same. Minimalism is a metaphor for brain improvement, but it's also a practical way to go about it.

The things in your home will keep staying the same if you don't make changes. Even if you aren't ready to make all these sacrifices yet, I challenge you to make some sacrifices. And don't just put some clothes in a bag to give away — really try to give away some things that you are hesitant to let go of.

If you challenge yourself to do this, I guarantee you that you'll forget what it was you gave away. When you reach that point, I want you to think of this book and how it told you to go even further. If you let go of more things, you wouldn't miss them. They would free you of more clutter, leaving you to focus on the important things in life.

Chapter 3: The Power of Feelings and Thoughts

You can find other resources that sell mp3 files for you to listen to that supposedly turn you into a genius. You can find vendors claiming to sell a milky drink that makes you smarter. You might notice something all these methods for brain improvement have in common —they are easy. Simply buy a drink, and you'll be smarter. Simply listen to some audio, and you'll be smarter.

Increasing your brainpower and getting smarter is not easy. You will have to set aside time and exert some effort. That is not to say that it will be hard, though. I am going to tell you an ancient Chinese proverb to illustrate what I mean.

A teacher calls upon three of his students. Before them, are three things: an empty bathtub, a well full of water, and a bucket with the bottom cut out. He assigns them a task. Fill the bathtub with water using the bucket. He leaves them to solve his riddle.

Two of the students are astonished that their teacher would tell them to do something impossible like this. They try to think of a way to do it, but the bucket has no bottom, and he told them they could not use anything else. Those two students eventually go home, having given up.

But the third students stayed for a bit after and thought of what she can do. When she holds the bucket on its side and dips it in the well, it can hold a very small amount of water. She can carefully bring the bucket to the tub and put the water in it.

She spends the rest of the night doing this, taking hundreds of trips between the well and the tub to fill the tub, little by little. By the time the sun comes up, the tub is full, and her teacher is pleased.

This proverb can apply to many things in life, but usually, it comes up in the context of learning. Just as little by little was the only way to fill the tub, little by little is the only way we can learn. We can't turn into geniuses by listening to audio files or drinking brain enhancers.

If we really want to become smarter, we have to be there for the whole journey, including the parts that we don't understand at first.

But this is important: just because you don't understand something at first, it does not mean you will never understand it. When you don't get something, take a deep breath and go over it again. If you still don't get it, walk away and take a break. Come back to it later. So many people never train themselves in subjects they could do well simply because they give up early.

Because of our previous experience and the brain connections we have already made, some things will come easier to us, and some harder. But the fact that you have any connections (which you do since you know how to read) means you are capable of learning.

I told you this proverb because we are going to spend a couple of pages talking about the biology of the brain, which might intimidate you if it's something you haven't been exposed to before. But you can learn this, too. Keep bringing the sideways bucket to the bathtub, and you'll get there eventually. The key to improving your brain is patience. Your path to a faster, smarter brain will require some patience.

The Microscopic Reality Behind Learning

Your brain is composed of cells called neurons, but these cells don't do anything useful on their own. The connections between them, called synapses, are forming all the time. The more time you spend learning, the more synaptic connections you form. On the smallest possible level, your synapses are what you change when you change your brain.

"Synapse" comes from the Greek word "synapsis," meaning "coming together." Your neurons come together to form synapses via electrical signals in your brain.

Throughout your brain, you have a mix of positive and negative electrical signals. Your neurons each have their own negative and positive charges. To form synapses, these opposite charges have to come together.

Altogether, your brain has more synapses than there are grains of sand on the beach — your brain has somewhere between ten and one hundred trillion synapses.

Each individual synapse is doing impressive work on its own. It learns when to fire based on new information, strengthening the more times it is used. If you know any skills or received an education, it was all possible thanks to your synapses. People with damage to the myelin sheath, the coating that makes it possible for your synapses to fire, usually end up having mental disorders.

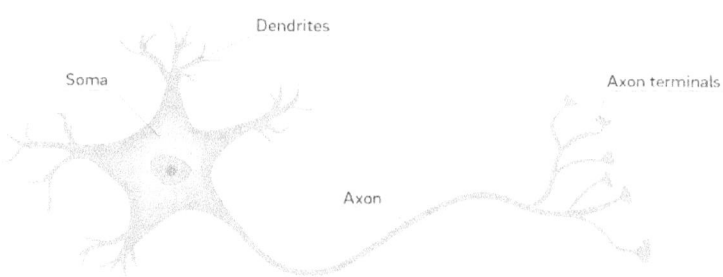

Image Courtesy of Medical Xpress

To recap, the biological term for the connections in your brain is "synapse." Synapses are microscopic signals your neurons send each other; synapses get stronger the more you fire them. If you fire a synapse enough, it becomes a prominent part of you.

But if you want to lose a synapse you don't like (be it a habit, behavior, or personality trait), all it takes is stopping those synapses from firing. If you do that, those connections will fade away (or prune) pretty quickly.

For now, our last lesson in the biology of the brain will be the major parts of the neuron that make synaptic connections possible. There are only a few you need to know.

The axon sends signals to neurons, and the dendrite receives signals from other neurons. The soma is the body of the neuron, containing the things all cells have, such as the nucleus, DNA, mitochondria, and so forth.

The neurons themselves can vary quite a bit, but the structure is always the same: an axon transmitter, a dendrite receiver, and a myelin sheath that speeds up the electrical pulses. While all neurons are microscopic, some look like typical cells in the rest of the body, while some of them are the length of a human leg!

Try to keep it clear in your mind that the axon, dendrite, soma, and myelin sheath are the physical parts that make synaptic connections possible. Synapses are not material — they are the electrical energy that is sent between neurons.

Synapses are where chemical messengers, called neurotransmitters, are sent between neurons. Neurotransmitters can't go directly from one neuron to the next, so the axons and dendrites of each neuron have to coordinate their messages every step of the way.

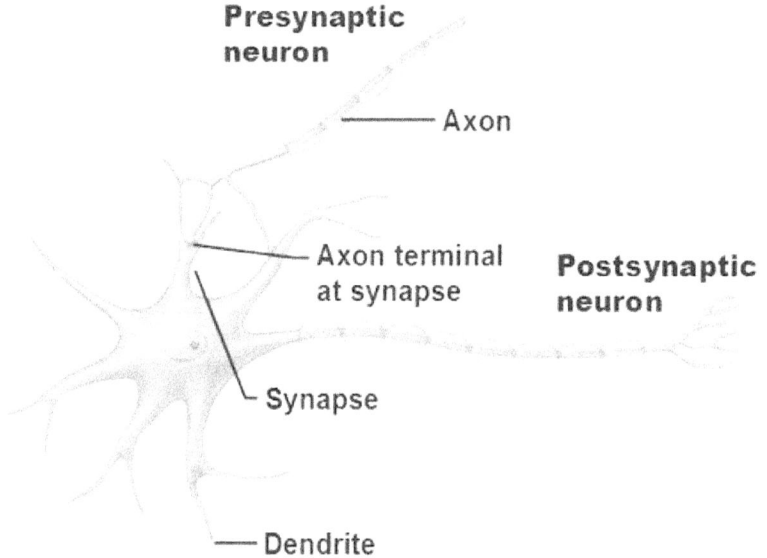

(a) Two neurons connected by synapses

Image Courtesy of Psychology Stack Exchange

Many different senders can pass on neurotransmitters to the dendrite of a neuron, and many different receivers can get neurotransmitters from the axon of a neuron. Sensory receptor cells can send a message to your neurons, teaching them to watch out for something in the environment in the future. Your neurons can send messages to your muscles to make them do something (at this very moment, your neurons are sending signals to your arms to hold up this book and to the muscles controlling your eyeballs to keep track of the words).

But your standard synapse lies between two neurons. The sender neuron is called the presynaptic neuron, and the receiver neuron is called the postsynaptic neuron.

The presynaptic neuron produces the neurotransmitters in the soma (the cell body) and transports the neurotransmitters to the postsynaptic neuron over the synaptic gap.

The following terms to describe this electrical signal all mean the same thing: synapse, synaptic connection, and synaptic gap. In science, we tend to call it the synaptic gap or the synaptic cleft because this connection happens in a space between neurons that is less than five-millionths of an inch in length.

Pretty much everything you experience, from extreme happiness to extreme sadness or confusion, is created in your brain in your electrochemical messaging system. The synapses communicate in two different ways depending on the situation, either chemically or electrically.

Electrical synapses happen immediately. They are used for things that should be brought to your attention right away. Chemical synapses take longer than electrical ones, but they are more precise. Electrical synapses reach many neurons in an area, while chemical synapses only target certain recipients. Electrical synapses fire so quickly because the signal never changes from its pure electrical state, allowing it to fire right away. Using an electrical synapse, a message can reach thousands of neurons at once.

Most of your synapses are chemical synapses, however. They are slower and send messages more selectively using chemical signals called neurotransmitters. Electrical synapses don't actually use neurotransmitters — they just use raw electricity. Neurotransmitters are more adaptable in a synapse than pure electricity. Neurons can control how quickly the neurotransmitters diffuse across the synaptic gap, and they can control whether they amplify or inhibit the signal.

In this book, I'll call them synapses when we are focusing on the biological side of things, and I'll just call them connections when we are applying what happens in your brain to your real life. But no matter what we call it, we are talking about the exact same thing.

I will refer to terms and ideas from this chapter later on but don't worry, by then you will have been introduced to them already, and we will be applying them practically to your real life. Not only will we be discussing biology with a more practical approach, but I will give you some quick refreshers, too. This stuff can undoubtedly be a little daunting if you are being introduced to it for the first time. But before you can unlock the vast potential of your brain, you have to know the fundamentals of its moving parts.

We won't spend too much more time on the details of the biology of synapses; we'll just explain enough so that you can visualize it. It is important that you understand the biological side, so you know exactly what it is you are training when you train your brain.

At this point, you must be wondering about the nature of neurotransmitters. What are they, and what kinds of neurotransmitters are there?

Every neurotransmitter has receptors in neurons that it bonds to. When they are close to neurons that have these receptors, the chemical reactions that result cause the neuron to be excited (please fire more!). When the neuron lacks the neurotransmitter's receptor, the resulting chemical reaction inhibits the neuron (please stop firing!).

You should know about the most essential neurotransmitters in your brain. They are:

Dopamine - Probably one of the most well-known of the neurotransmitters, dopamine works with other neurotransmitters to regulate behavior. Your neurons use dopamine to create movements as a reaction to emotion. It is most famous for being the "reward chemical," though, giving you a pleasant rush of dopamine every time you engage in behavior that gives you a reward. Your brain has learned over the years that ice cream is delicious. When you put a spoonful in your mouth, not only do you experience the pleasure of vanilla nut, but you feel dopamine surging through your brain. It's trying to tell you, Keep doing this. This is good. You love that dopamine reward, so it makes you more likely to indulge in sweets in the future.

Serotonin - Another one of the most famous neurotransmitters, serotonin has a number of functions, but it is commonly thought of as the "feel-good chemical." People without enough serotonin feel sleepy, have less energy, and have thought patterns associated with depression. Serotonin is heavily involved in behavior, mood, sleep, and even digestion. Recent scientific discoveries have shown that 60% of the serotonin in your brain is actually produced in the gut. Before, neuroscientists thought that serotonin was sealed off in the brain, being produced exclusively there and not occurring anywhere else. The discovery of this strong link between the gut and serotonin makes it seem there is a lot of truth in the phrase, "You are what you eat." There are many new books you can find in the growing field of gut science, and I recommend that you give them a look. It may just tip the balance of your mood in your favor. Without oversimplifying the challenges many of us have in dealing with our emotions, this breakthrough in the study of serotonin highlights how necessary it is to eat healthful foods. Besides eating well, there are several ways you can regulate the levels of serotonin in your brain. You should take time every day to go outside and breathe fresh air, exercise a few times a week, and sleep at least seven hours every night.

Acetylcholine - A vital actor in the nervous system, this neurotransmitter works with neurons that control your motor functions and your muscles. Your motor neurons send acetylcholine to your muscles to make you sit up in your chair, stretch your legs, hold up this book, and so on. Acetylcholine is the only neurotransmitter that goes to your voluntary muscles; any conscious choice you make to move your body uses acetylcholine. When you are aware of your breathing, acetylcholine is playing the role of the messenger between the brain and body. Acetylcholine also plays a role in cognitive functions like memory and attention.

GABA - GABA stands for gamma-aminobutyric acid. This neurotransmitter goes between the brain and the nervous system and helps your neurons communicate with one another. It is an inhibitory neurotransmitter, so it tells your neurons not to fire. Some people take GABA supplements to help them with stress, anxiety, and depression. It helps with these problems because often, individuals with symptoms of anxiety and depression have too many synapses going off, making them stressed and unable to function normally. There are many similar drugs, including antidepressants, that change how neurotransmitters release or block your neurotransmitter's receptors. Your body produces GABA naturally, though, so you can avoid taking unnecessary supplements by following along in the book and learn how to expertly make use of chemicals you already have. GABA stands in contrast to glutamate, which causes neurons to fire. What they have in common is that they exclusively cause neurons to either fire or not fire. Other neurotransmitters can cause either to happen. GABA and glutamate are also the most abundant neurotransmitters in your brain — GABA is found in 40% of synapses, while glutamate is part of 50% of synapses. It might seem strange for an inhibitory neurotransmitter to be so present in the brain, but without GABA, the neurons in our brains would fire synapses far too often and overwhelm us.

Glutamate - As we said before, while GABA tells neurons not to fire, glutamate tells them to fire. We need both of these neurotransmitters to have a balance between stimulation and overstimulation. Without GABA, we may lose track of all the information we gather from our senses and lose the ability to focus. But without glutamate, we would find it harder to build more synaptic connections. We wouldn't have the "push" that glutamate gives us. For this reason, glutamate is an important player in memory.

Norepinephrine - Along with the neurotransmitter cortisol, norepinephrine is known as a stress chemical. It is involved in multiple aspects of your behavior, regulating mood and arousal. Norepinephrine peaks when you are in stressful or dangerous situations, preparing you to act. When you have this much norepinephrine in your body, you breathe more efficiently, taking in more oxygen to the brain. This helps you think more clearly since your brain relies on oxygen as much as any other part of your body. (You might be surprised to hear the brain uses 20% of your body's oxygen.) For the same purpose, this neurotransmitter makes your heartbeat faster, allocating more blood to your muscles in case you need to use them. What's most fascinating is that norepinephrine temporarily disables your digestive system, so they don't take up so much of your energy. When your norepinephrine surges, instead of using blood and energy on digestion, they are used to make you prepared for a fight-or-flight response. Any time you are in fight-or-flight mode, norepinephrine is doing its job of getting you ready for whatever you decide to do. Whether you engage the threat or run away from it, your body will be able to do what it has to.

The science journal High Existence explains how neurotransmitters shape our thoughts and feelings through the division of neuron cells:

There are thousands upon thousands of receptors on each cell in our body. Each receptor is specific to one peptide, or protein. When we have feelings of anger, sadness, guilt, excitement, happiness, or nervousness, each separate emotion releases its own flurry of neuropeptides. Those peptides surge through the body and connect with those receptors which change the structure of each cell as a whole. Where this gets interesting is when the cells actually divide. If a cell has been exposed to a certain peptide more than others, the new cell that is produced through its division will have more of the receptor that matches that specific peptide. Likewise, the cell will also have fewer receptors for peptides that its mother/sister cell was not exposed to as often.

The proteins (or neuropeptides) are the parts of neurotransmitters that are bonded to the receptors in our neurons. When a lot of the neurotransmitter serotonin goes through our brains because we found a way to let go and be happy, serotonin will be more likely to surge through our bodies in the future.

This is because when serotonin bonds with your neurons, it changes their structure. When these changed neurons divide to make new neurons, the new neurons have more receptors for serotonin.

This means letting yourself be happy today will literally make it easier for you to get happy later. This is not to say that you can just force yourself to be happy. But the takeaway you should have is this: when you have the opportunity to let go of your worries and be happy in the moment, take it. Sometimes it is harder than others, but if you push yourself to be happy more often, you will be doing your future self a favor.

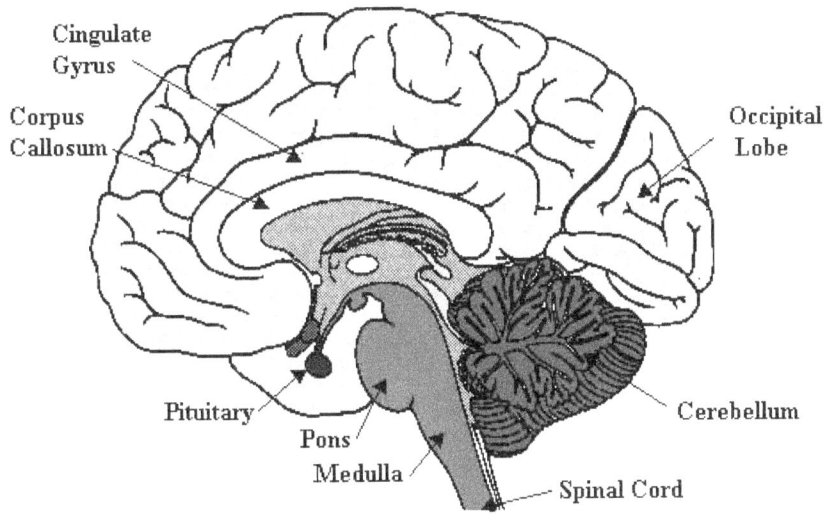

Image Courtesy of Washington University

Your Brain Parts and You

The human brain is about the size of a grapefruit, which is three times the brain size of mammals about the same overall size as humans. It is protected from trauma by your skull.

Your brain contains four main lobes. The parietal lobe is in charge of your experience of touch; the temporal lobe allows you to hear; your occipital lobe allows you to see; finally, your frontal lobe is in charge of your thinking. These lobes are all part of the cerebrum, which is the thinking part of the brain.

Your brain has other functions that we share with all animals. Your cerebellum allows you to do physical activities like play sports. The cerebellum is situated in the lower part of your brain, right next to the brain stem.

Your brain stem has its own purpose, too. It regulates your balance, sleepiness, heart rate, swallowing, and breathing. It does all the most basic things your body must do in order to keep going.

It's good for you to know all of these parts and their functions, but the parts that concern us the most in this book are all in the cerebrum. Your cerebrum gets input and makes sense of this information. It's the reason you are able to make sense of the symbols on this page. Using your trillions of synapses, the cerebrum makes sense of things and puts them together.

One fascinating aspect of our cerebrum is how it will even put things together that do not go together. It does not like it when we don't complete us.

In your head, you just filled in the word "sentences." It happened automatically. That was your higher-level thought processing at work. But there are many examples of times you wouldn't want your brain to fill in blanks.

Have you ever heard people about ten feet away from you and thought they were talking about you? You didn't know for sure, and you couldn't hear them very well, but you caught a few words here and there. All the complex synapses you have in the cerebrum were able to make sense out of very little information.

But the big disadvantage to the way your brain makes sense of things is that it doesn't really know what is true. All it can do is run with the limited information it has and make a story out of it. This story might not be accurate, but all your brain cares about is painting a full picture, because it doesn't like uncertainty. The truth is, those people probably weren't talking about you at all.

If you thought they were talking about you, that probably had more to do with what was going on in your own mind. You might have had connections in your brain that reflected your insecurities — and when you heard some people saying words that sounded a bit like your name, you put the sounds that seemed like your name together with your own insecurities. Like magic, it seemed like people were talking about you when they almost definitely were not.

This is a key point when becoming more aware of your brain and the work it does for you: it puts things together that don't always go together. As long as it can piece together some kind of story, some kind of full picture, that's all it cares about.

Without a doubt, your brain is an amazing piece of biological machinery. But a thought occurring to your head doesn't make it true. Sometimes, your brain fills in the gaps with anything it can find because it doesn't like leaving things incomplete. It doesn't like leaving things as unknowns.

Maybe you aren't familiar with machine learning, but the way your brain learns is really not so different from this field in computer science. In machine learning, the programmer gives new inputs to a program so it can learn from them. The more inputs a machine learning program is given, the closer it gets to the answer that it needs.

In much the same way, your brain makes new synapses when it is given new inputs. If you want your brain to grow into a machine that can perform a wide variety of tasks, you have to keep giving it new inputs. You can't expect to improve your brain if you continue to give your brain inputs that it is already comfortable with. It has to be given a challenge.

It is like how many English teachers would say: "The truth comes out of conflict." New subjects will always be a conflict for your brain because it wants to understand things. It doesn't like not understanding things. But if you push yourself to stick with new challenges, you allow your connections to multiply, making you more intelligent.

The cerebrum is the most highly connected part of your brain. It is what scientists refer to when they talk about the right and left hemispheres (although the idea of a left and right brain is outdated and no longer accepted, our brains are still divided into two hemispheres connected by the corpus callosum).

Your brain stem may be the most directly involved in breathing and swallowing, but your cerebrum has connections to these functions, too. When you are aware of your breathing, your cerebrum is doing work because you are making yourself conscious of it. Anytime you are aware or conscious of something, that is activity in your cerebrum.

It contains what we call the mammalian and rational brains. The mammalian brain is a structure of the brain that we share with all mammals; it is the part of the brain where emotions are processed. The rational brain takes up far more space; we are the only species with the rational brain.

The rational brain includes the neocortex. The cerebrum takes up the most space in the whole brain, and the neocortex takes up the most space in the cerebrum. It is called the neocortex because it is the newest part of the brain; in humans, the neocortex is particularly advanced. It takes up about 90% of our brains, which is a far greater proportion than any other animal. It contains all the synaptic connections we make as a result of our interactions with our environment.

Besides the neocortex, the cerebrum contains other structures with very specific functions. The cerebrum has a few structures that perform highly specific tasks that our brains have evolved to do. One of these is the hypothalamus.

The hypothalamus is only the size of a cornel of corn, but it helps you balance and controls your body temperature. It is also connected to your pituitary gland, which releases hormones in your body. Since the hypothalamus is heavily involved with the gland that releases hormones, it should come as no surprise that the hypothalamus is greatly associated with the emotion of anger.

While the cerebrum has rational and emotional brains, we actually have a third "brain" called the reptilian brain which operates in the brain stem. An animal's reptilian brain is what conducts the tasks of breathing, swallowing, and other basic functions. It is a very small part of the brain compared to the others, but it is no less important. If you neglect your basic needs for food, water, and oxygen, it will be impossible for you to achieve greater goals.

Most of this book is about improving the higher parts of your brain in the cerebrum, but we will spend a little bit of time talking about listening to your reptilian brain too. I am sure you already know how important physical health is to brain health, but we need to emphasize this point because it is just that important. If you neglect your most basic needs, you can't expect to achieve higher aims.

At the end of the day, the majority of your brain is the cerebrum. It is involved in higher functions that let you think through math problems, learn new things, use fine motor control, do abstract thought, and use logic, but it also lets you make associations between your senses and meanings.

If there is a particular food that you associate with a bad memory, the smell of that food will make your cerebrum fire all of the synapses related to that memory. Your brain is an incredible network of connections like this, and those connections are all housed in the cerebrum.

It allows you to have fine motor control, as well. You don't remember now, but when you were a kid, you had to learn how to flip a light switch. It comes naturally to you now, so much so that you can't even imagine why you wouldn't be able to do that. But the action of flipping a light switch is actually something that requires some degree of fine motor control. The same goes for holding a fork or opening a can of soda.

Fine motor control like this doesn't come from the cerebellum or the brainstem; it is a skill that you must learn. Any skill that you learn has connections in the cerebrum. These connections are so well carved into our brains that we can't imagine living our lives without them.

We've talked a lot about forging new synaptic connections in your brain, and now you know where those connections go: in the cerebrum, which takes up the bulk of the space in your brain.

This is very exciting because it means the largest, most important part of your brain is also the most manipulable. You can change it through your own behaviors. You can change your behaviors by learning new habits.

The rest of the book will get into how you practically go about starting new habits. Once you have these habits integrated into your daily life, they will show up in your cerebrum as strong synaptic connections that won't easily go away.

You should see the light at the end of the tunnel now: you should see the clear path towards your new brain, your new self. You know how it works biologically, so you know that it is not a dream, but a very real possibility.

Scientists call the brain the most fascinating thing we have discovered in the universe. While there are still new discoveries being made about it and we don't understand everything about the brain, there are also many earth-shattering discoveries that have already been made. There are things we do understand about the brain, and that is the focus of this book. We know enough to operate it like experts and construct our own mental operating systems.

There are many things I hope you have learned from this chapter, but if there is one thing I want you to come to believe by now, it is this: our brains literally get smarter the more we use them. We are born knowing nothing. Every so-called smart person got to be that way by gradually and patiently learning. Your brain follows all the same biological principles as theirs do, so you are entirely capable of becoming smart the same way.

Chapter 4: You Are Your Habits

Making Yourself Familiar with Your Own Brain Patterns

If you're picking up a book about training and improving your brain, there are probably a slew of reasons for it. But whether you want to get smarter, improve your memory, satisfy your thirst for knowledge, or all of the above, you will have to take what we learned about the brain and apply it to your own behavior. You will have to monitor your habits on a deep, cerebral level to achieve this.

The electricity that pulses through your brain occurs in patterns. In real life, these electrical patterns make up your habits. Do you have a habit of playing with your hair or slouching? The only reason you do these things is because you wired your brain to do them.

It may be hard to think back to when these habits started, but science tells us that it only takes about four weeks to make or break a habit. Your habits make you, so if you want to create a new self, you have to create new habits.

As someone who wants to better themselves, you likely already have enough smarts to get by. But one quote by Aristotle comes to mind: "The more you know, the more you know you don't know." The quest for skills and information never ends, because the more you hone and acquire, the more previously unknown paths you can follow.

Your brain doesn't simply store knowledge in different compartments. Everything you know, you can access because of the thousands of connections between your neurons. There are always unknown paths to explore because there are always new synapses to be born.

Altogether, these new synapses can form new skills, habits, and even personality traits. If you behave in new ways, you make new synapses. If you read about subjects you wouldn't normally read about, you make new synapses, and they connect with your older ones to make your understanding richer than before.

You might have read the title of this book and thought to yourself: can the brain really be made smarter?

Yes, it can. Your intelligence is not set in stone. Your brain is a collection of trillions of connections between your neurons. Every time you learn something new, this arrangement of connections changes, changing your brain.

Neuroplasticity is the term scientists use to describe how the brain can drastically change depending on your environment and the inputs you give it.

If you plan to use this book to become smarter, you will have to adopt a growth mindset of learning. In developmental psychology, the growth mindset refers to the belief that your intelligence is not fixed and can be changed. The fixed mindset of learning is the opposite — it is the belief that you are as smart as you are and can never change.

The fixed mindset is closely tied to the idea of IQ. People have many misconceptions about IQ but addressing them will require us to define intelligence.

Simply put, intelligence is the ability to learn new things and adapt to new situations. IQ tests measure baseline knowledge, problem-solving, working memory, math, and visualization of objects. We can see that the test measures some things that are associated with intelligence, but it hardly seems comprehensive.

There are a lot of issues with the idea that IQ measures pure intelligence. In one study, half of the participants were given ten dollars to take an IQ test, while the other half were not given any money. The participants who got money scored on average 20 points higher on the IQ test.

The first IQ test was made in France in 1900 because of a new egalitarian law requiring all children to attend school to learn basics like reading, math, science, and history. It was anticipated that children would be at different starting points in their learning, so rather than group students by age, they took an IQ test written by Alfred Binet.

The test was never meant to measure "innate intelligence," but to measure where kids were now so they could be placed in classroom environments that would best suit their needs. But somehow the myth persists that all of us are born into a certain level of intelligence.

Decades of research have shown that the growth mindset of learning leads to higher scores on intelligence tests. In classrooms where teachers used the growth mindset in their class, students scored higher on these tests.

We know that intelligence can change. In this book, you will improve your intelligence in a straightforward, practical way.

To frame how we think about intelligence, we will discuss the nine "intelligences" from Howard Gardner's book Frames of Mind: The Theory of Multiple Intelligences. In his book, Gardner wrote that a fixed number such as IQ could not describe someone's intelligence. He said the human mind had a number of capacities; the bits of intelligence he named were musical-rhythmic, visual-spatial, verbal-linguistic, logical-mathematical, bodily-kinesthetic, interpersonal, intrapersonal, naturalistic, and existential-moral.

Your brain has enormous potential in all of these areas. Because of the neuroplasticity of your brain, you will become smarter the more you can make connections between all of these areas. In this chapter, we will make ourselves familiar with each of them.

I want you to think about what your strengths are and what you could improve on. But keep in mind that Gardner himself said these "intelligences" were not meant to limit people. They were meant to empower people to grow intellectually.

If you excel in one area, you are just as capable of excelling in another. After all, from the perspective of the brain, learning any skill or area of knowledge looks exactly the same — it looks like clusters of neurons connected by synapses.

Don't limit yourself and define yourself by the areas you already do well in. Realize that you can build connections in logical-mathematical intelligence just like you did with your verbal-linguistic intelligence, and vice-versa.

People have a tendency to pick a few specialties and use them to build an identity. There is nothing wrong with this, but don't let your identity as an outdoorsman keep you from improving your people skills. Don't let your identity as a philosopher stop you from using your muscles.

Your brain is plastic — moldable. It's not your "natural gifts" and "natural weaknesses" that stop you from learning new things. It's your belief that your brain is set in stone and is only wired for certain things.

Your brain — you — can do anything. As corny as that might sound, it's true. Neuroscientists have been trying to tell us for years that our brains become whatever we put into them.

With this scientifically backed growth mindset of learning, you should explore these different intelligences and think about how they fit into your life right now.

If you think some of these bits of intelligence barely have a place in your life, think of how you could change that. There are so many possibilities for what you can learn and become. If you see yourself strictly as an artist today, imagine yourself in the future holding a conversation about black holes.

You can get to a point where you master multiple fields of knowledge. This version of you will be a fountain of conversation topics, making you a person that others want to be around. Being someone who knows about a lot of different things simply makes you more interesting than someone who sticks to one thing they know.

If your brain was scanned in an fMRI machine, the scientist would tell you that you have many synapses going off. You will rely on other people for knowledge less and find that people are coming to you.

Your brain is a machine with moving parts made of synapses and cells instead of cogs and gears. If we want to make a manmade machine produce more things, we build upon it. We get more parts and put them together, making a new machine.

Building upon your brain is easier. You already have the neurons. Just use them in new ways, and they'll come together to make synapses like a game of connect-the-dots. The more dots (or neurons) that connect, the closer you come to a realization that changes your way of thinking.

The best way to brainstorm what budding talents you should improve on is by looking at the profiles of these different intelligences. After all, these are virtually all the things that your brain is capable of.

Try to imagine yourself being described as each of them. Don't only brainstorm ways you can improve your abilities in these bits of intelligence individually but make connections between all of them — connect musical-rhythmic intelligence with interpersonal; connect verbal-linguistic intelligence with naturalistic.

Musical-rhythmic intelligence

If you already have a knack for music, you can memorize and repeat the pitch. You recognize instruments in music you hear. You notice when someone is singing off-key or clapping off the beat. A musically and rhythmically intelligent person plays an instrument, whether it is the piano, trumpet, or human voice. Becoming more adept in musical-rhythmic intelligence means becoming more like this person. How can you make music a larger part of your life?

Visual-spatial intelligence

Spatial intelligence is your ability to understand shapes in 3D space. If you are a visual learner, you might have a high level of visual-spatial intelligence. Maybe you find physics easy to understand, or you are an avid artist. You have a close to a photographic memory and are good with maps. Improving in this area demands that we spend a lot of time in our imagination trying to conjure images in our heads. Bring these images to life by working on your drawing skills.

Verbal-linguistic intelligence

A person with high verbal-linguistic intelligence is highly sensitive to the sonic dimension of words; they are able to name what makes a group of words sound good. They make good speakers, listeners, writers, and readers. Since you're already a reader, I bet you already have a lot of confidence in this area. But you can get even better by having conversations with strangers and writing in a journal every day.

Logical-mathematical intelligence

This intelligence describes a person's ability to use reason and make connections between things. The mathematical component describes our ability to use numbers and apply them to science and the real world. You can improve these connections by playing logic games, playing number games, and learning the basics of computer programming.

Bodily-kinesthetic intelligence

People with strong bodily-kinesthetic intelligence are highly aware of their bodies; their fine and gross motor skills are more advanced than the average person's. They tend to use their bodies to communicate with people. To improve this intelligence, learn practical household skills like fixing a bathtub to develop your muscle memory. It will strengthen the link between your brain and the rest of your body.

Interpersonal intelligence

Interpersonally intelligent people are highly effective communicators, able to understand what people want and convey their own thoughts effectively. They are sensitive to emotions, which makes this intelligence highly related to emotional intelligence. These people enjoy being around others more than anything else. If you want to improve your interpersonal skills, you will have to spend more time around new people and improve upon the relationships you already have.

Intrapersonal intelligence

People with high intrapersonal intelligence are very self-aware and reflective. This sort of intelligence tends to go with verbal-linguistic intelligence because someone who is self-aware is better able to express their thoughts and feelings in words. You will still want to spend time with people to hone your interpersonal intelligence, but to improve this one, you should also set aside time to be with just yourself without any noise. Let yourself think about whatever comes to your mind. You might come across thoughts you never noticed before.

Naturalistic intelligence

People with naturalistic intelligence know a lot about plants and animals. They know the creatures who dwell in their area and often take time to enjoy the sunset. This intelligence can be easy to lose track of in our tech-focused society, but since we are part of nature too, it is important that we get back in touch with it.

Existential-moral intelligence

The most philosophical of the bits of intelligence, one's existential-moral intelligence describes their values and how they relate to the vast universe. It includes their sense of right and wrong and how they believe they fit in the world. Being more existentially and morally intelligent doesn't necessarily mean adopting specific lifestyles or ideals. We just have to keep asking the big questions as we live out our lives.

The starting point for all knowledge is memorizing rote information, but if you truly want to improve your brain, you will have to make connections between these intelligences. The harder the connections are to see, the more important they are to improve your brain. This is because when the connection is less obvious, your brain must think creatively.

To help you when you actually start to learn new skills based on these bits of intelligence, I want to briefly give you some advice about learning. It boils down to a studying tip that is told to every high-achieving student: if you want to do well on a test, it doesn't matter how "hard" you study for it. It doesn't even matter how many hours you study it. The thing that will really affect your score is how many times you set aside a period of time to study for the test and did some meaningful studying.

Knowing what you know now about how your synapses work, the usefulness of this advice should come as no surprise to you. After all, you could keep firing the same synapse over an over by thinking through the same memory for an hour, but if you don't pay that memory a visit the next day, the synapse isn't going to get particularly strong.

But if you think about the same memory for five minutes every day for a month, it is basically a permanent part of you. And it's a part of you that won't go away unless you go about another month without thinking about it. Not thinking about it won't be easy, either, because it's now a prominent part of you. Your brain picks up on patterns like this really well. It does okay at remembering things that are repeated vigorously in a long session, but it does phenomenally at remembering things that you do every day.

You can even use this knowledge with negative thoughts. If you have the same negative thoughts every day, add some positive thoughts to that routine. The negative ones won't go away right away, but now you have some positive thoughts alongside them. If you reinforce the positive thoughts more than the negative ones, eventually the negative ones will be replaced.

One last learning tip for studying a new bit of intelligence is to write. Words are the building blocks of thought. Our brains might not always think in eloquent sentences, but if you jot down what's on your mind, you can work through your thoughts and feelings logically.

If you can't just put your thoughts in words, it's not much of a thought at all. It's an intuition, an instinct.

Intuitions and instincts are fine, but they are only starting points. You want to reach the finish line, which you will arrive at by forming fully fleshed-out sentences that describe what you are thinking.

It is hard to organize your thoughts in words, without a doubt. But if you don't put words to them, it's like your brain is stuck at the beginning of a story. You can't get to the rising action after the conflict because you don't know what choice you are making. You haven't fully reasoned out what is on your mind.

This is part of being human, but you need a tool for getting past this stage of thought. And that tool is a pen. As poet Seamus Heaney wrote:

The squat pen rests.
I'll dig with it.

The conventional idea is that a number can describe someone's intelligence. The fact that people still believe this is pretty incredible, isn't it? It shows how powerful ideas can be when enough people believe them.

Turning our backs to this debunked and outmoded idea of intelligence, let's embrace Gardner's notion of multiple intelligences and see for ourselves that making creative connections between them will train our brains.

Chapter 5: Silencing your Mind and Being Present

How to Free Yourself with Mindfulness Meditation

Changing your habits might seem impossible. Your habits have basically hypnotized you into thinking that they can't be changed — but they can absolutely be changed.

Take a moment to clear out all of the distractions in your environment. Anything with a screen or a speaker, remove it from the room or remove yourself. Take time to notice all the things that run through your head that you cover up with noise.

You will realize many of the same thoughts keep occurring to you. You will become more aware of the things that make you. Reaching this point is an indescribably freeing experience.

When was the last time you really let yourself do this? If you're being honest with yourself, I would bet that you haven't done this in a year. Maybe longer.

And there's no way that is good for you. It's not good for you to just go, go, go. When are the times that you will reflect if you never stop to allow yourself to do it?

You are not a machine. I know that we have talked a lot about how your brain is like a biological machine. But it is not a literal machine made out of wires and silicon. You are a delicate, nature-created machine that needs a lot of maintenance and care.

One of my mindfulness meditation coaches once explained it so perfectly: in our culture, we are always filling ourselves with things. We are not only filling ourselves with consumption, like with foods, drinks, and sugar. We are also filling ourselves with mass media and entertainment, with work and the stresses that come along with it.

You can't expect to stay healthy if all you do is put more things into yourself. You also need to leave time every day where you can empty yourself out.

That is what being present is all about. When you are present, you do nothing but sit with yourself and observe what happens. You observe what is true. You come across what is true by not letting your mind get cluttered with more information. You filled most of your day by putting ideas and emotions in your mind. Now you need to give yourself time to loosen up.

A common mistake with meditation is that people use the time to think about what is stressing themselves out. It is very similar to not being able to go to bed because you keep going through the events of the day, and the things that you will have to do the next day. When you meditate, much like when you sleep, you have to stop letting the planning and reminiscing distract you from the present.

If you have not already established a meditation practice in your life, you may be curious as to how you can implement meditation in a powerful way. Meditation is a great mindfulness practice, and it can be extremely easy to begin meditating on a regular basis. The key is learning to work with your mind.

Meditation is a practice that we must establish and grow on our own terms. Like other skills, some people will pick it up and do phenomenally right away, and others will have to take their time and build their skill. This is not something that you can compare with others or compete with others on. Instead, it is something that you have to build within yourself. When it comes to meditation, some days it will be easy and others it will not. Typically, on the days when it is not easy you can confirm that those will be the days when you need it the most. On the days when it is easy, practice anyway.

One of the most common questions is whether or not there is a right or wrong way to meditate. Often times, people think they are doing something incorrectly because the mind has that tendency to wander. People find ways to question just about everything from the position they are into the way their hands rest. Like we discussed in step five above, recognizing the thought and then returning to the meditation technique (which we will discuss later), is all you need to do. If you are able to acknowledge that thought, put it back where it belongs and continue with your practice, then you are doing it right.

Another question is if it is necessary to practice every day. The answer to that is no, but if you expect to get good at mindful meditation, you will want to practice as often as possible. The more you do it, the more beneficial it becomes. Not only that, the more often you practice, the easier it becomes. It will also be a part of your daily routine because you've found where it fits into your schedule perfectly every day. Studies have shown that it takes about twenty-eight days to make a habit of something. Think of mindful meditation that way. Get through twenty-eight consecutive days of meditation and you have formed a healthy habit!

Finally, the third most common question has to do with the formality of mindfulness practice. Really, it can be done alone or in a group at any time and any place. If group activities don't appeal to you, that's okay too. Reading this book will guide you toward your solo practice. And, if you find you'd like to try group meditation a try, there are tons of resources online. It's pretty likely there is a group near you!

Your habits can be changed; you have to stop being stampeded by your old thought patterns. You created the ones that are distracting you now, so you can create new ones that will make life easier for you in the future.

Stop creating new thoughts that will make life harder for you in the future. Your thoughts stick with you for a long time. They aren't permanent, which is why they can change, but they do last. If you are going to move on from your old self and retrain your brain to become something it has never been before, you will have to do a lot of letting go.

You can think about the future but think about the future in new ways. Stop following your same old patterns of imagining the worst possible outcome — or maybe you don't imagine the worst possible outcome, but you imagine "same old, same old." You never imagine that things can be different or new.

They can be different and new, and it all has to start with your own mind.

I told you to remove the noisy distractions from your environment. But you can be one of those distractions, too. What are the loudest thoughts in your head? Look away from the page for a second and really ask yourself this question. Which thoughts keep coming up the most?

Maybe you have thoughts that keep trying to creep up, but you repress them. They are not "allowed" in your mind. Well, it is your own mind. No harm will come from simply hearing what the thought is. So, hear it.

You can free yourself by hearing out your mind only, but it will only work if you follow this advice. Listen to what is true and don't get slowed down by old patterns.

Your old patterns are exactly what you need to let go of if you want to change. We talked through the different possible intelligences that you can learn. What was the intelligence that you already associated yourself with? What was the intelligence that you wish you had, but you don't think you do? Take this time to think of yourself as a person with that intelligence.

You are fundamentally no different from someone with this intelligence. If you want to become more like this person, all you have to do is keep thinking more like they do. If you want to be a more musical-rhythmic individual, think about a song that you like. How does the melody go? You might find that even if you can't do all the right pitches, you can "hear" it in your own head.

Music is amazing this way: neuroscientists have found that when we listen to music, it activates synapses all across the brain. This is why music therapy is a new option that a lot of nursing homes are considering for patients with Alzheimer's. Sometimes when patients with Alzheimer's listen to music from their adolescence, they light up and open up about their old memories. They act like completely different people from the ones who they normally do.

Try to think of yourself in a similar way. You may not be someone with Alzheimer's Disease, but you can think of times where something happened that triggered a memory. Have you ever driven down an old road from your childhood and it made you think of your old school days? Have you ever had the most random thoughts come across your head, and you had no idea why?

Even if you didn't know why the thought occurred to you, it was probably because your brain noticed something in your environment that reminded you of it.

Music is a great example of this phenomenon. Have you ever started humming a song you like out of nowhere? Then you thought back to earlier when you were watching TV, and you realize that very song played in a commercial.

Our memories are summoned by cues in our environment. Many of us do not think much about it, but it is true. While our memories are still in our brains when they are not being triggered in the form of a synapse, they will not occur to us unless the proper stimulus causes us to think about them.

You can see this with your emotions. We will go back to talking about parts of your brain for a moment so we can talk about emotion.

You may have heard of the amygdala before. If you have read anything about the way emotions work in the brain before, you definitely saw something about the amygdala. Pronounced uh-mig-duh-luh, this almond-shaped brain part is what triggers your emotions.

But of course, your brain doesn't have you feel emotions just for the sake of it. They evolved to be what they are now because of the evolutionary purpose they had for our ancestors. For our ancestors, the amygdala was very important for survival. When they were near danger, like if they were near a larger creature that could harm them, the amygdala would activate. This would trigger a fear response in old humans, and the human would have a fight-or-flight response. (In this case, it would probably be a flight response.)

You would have the same reaction today. If a large, scaly monster crashed into your living room window, your amygdala would activate. You wouldn't have to logically figure out what you need to do, because your amygdala would do all that work for you.

The thing that makes it so hard for modern humans is that we don't have to worry about these life-or-death scenarios as much as we used to, yet we still have an amygdala. Personally, I am still glad I have an amygdala in case I ever do have to fend for my life. But it can be challenging to cope with times that the amygdala goes off when it doesn't need to.

Now, why would the amygdala activate unnecessarily? You might be asking yourself this question, but you have already experienced this for yourself. Do you have any irrational fears, be it social situations or anything of that nature? When you are around the thing that stimulates this fear response, the feeling you get is a result of your amygdala. If you want your amygdala to stop being so sensitive, you have to change how you physically respond to your own feelings.

The reason we are talking about the amygdala is this: it is an excellent example of a situation where you would want to change your brain patterns. Just like any brain pattern, the way you have trained your amygdala was learned, and you can unlearn it.

Your irrational fears may be stimuli that cause a fear response in the amygdala, but you can also create new stimuli that accompany that stimulus. You can't just pretend that your learned fear isn't there; it is still there and pretending it isn't will not help you unlearn it. Your only option is to have positive thoughts alongside the anxiety-inducing ones that the amygdala gives you.

You are responsible for being your own stimulus, sometimes. With matters of improving your brain, this is something that you have to take care of yourself. There is no way you can take a pill that completely solves this for you. The only option is to face it head-on.

But your emotions are a physical experience. Maybe they seemed mysterious to you at first, but now you know that your fear is harbored in a brain part called the amygdala. Now you know that when you are scared, your amygdala was activated because you taught it that you were afraid of something. Teaching your amygdala not to trigger in these moments will require you to change your mental models.

The name itself gives you a good idea of what a mental model is, but here is the run-down. We all have our beliefs about the world. We have ideas about what different things are and what properties they have. For example, we know that dogs have four legs and that skunks smell bad. Once we have these ideas about these categories, it is hard to change how we see them.

But like I told you in chapter three, our brains do not have direct knowledge of the truth. Instead, they take the limited information they have and construct stories out of that information.

If your amygdala is going off because you are anxious about being around people, this is because your mental model of people includes how scary they are. If you want to teach your amygdala that actually, people are not scary, you have to change the way you act around people. After your amygdala has seen that you are acting normal around people and not anxious, it will stop firing.

The example of the amygdala is just one where we can see that our subjective experiences are really physical when you get right down to it. The more you spend time with yourself and observe your mental world, the closer you will be to this truth. You are your brain, and your brain is the inputs you have put into it so far. Simply add new inputs despite the old ones that make it hard. If you keep at it, you will build a new self that is entirely your own.

Mindfulness Meditation Practice

It is finally time for us to practice doing some actual mindfulness meditation practice. The first thing you have to do is find a quiet place. If there is anyone in your home, get to a room where you can have peace and quiet. Keep the lights dim and don't bring your phone with you. You are now ready to do mindfulness meditation.

We already talked about what this kind of meditation is, so we are not going to focus so much on the definitions now. We are going to focus on actually doing it. The most classic form of mindfulness meditation is also the most popular: you are going to focus on your breath and only your breath.

Sit with your legs crossed and give yourself something to lean back on. You don't want to lie down, because you don't want to fall asleep. You want to be awake for this so you can observe yourself.

For a couple of minutes, all I want you to do is breathe. Don't overthink this part, because it doesn't even matter what you think about at the beginning of mindfulness meditation. Forget anything you have heard about clearing your mind for now. We will get there, but you don't have to worry about it yet.

Breathe in through your nose and out through your mouth. If you do that, you are doing everything correctly so far. Now we can get to the next part, which has to do with what you are focusing on.

It is inevitable that you think about other things, and the reason is what we have already discussed — your brain has hundreds of trillions of synapses! Of course, they constantly fire. If only 1% of your connections were firing, that would still be trillions of synapses.

This is why you don't have to worry about intentionally clearing your mind — it would be a silly goal.

You can't get yourself to stop thinking with sheer force. It's like the joke about not thinking about the pink elephant. If someone tells you not to think about a pink elephant, any attempt not to think about it is pointless.

If you are intentionally trying not to think about the pink elephant, you have to keep in the back of your mind not to think about it. Inevitably, this will keep the pink elephant in your mind.

The real way you clear your mind is illustrated well in the proverb I told you at the beginning of the third chapter. You have to bring the sideways bucket to the bathtub one trip at a time. There is no quick and easy way to do it. With meditation, taking it slowly and patiently takes the form of focusing on your breath.

Focus on your breath, and only your breath. When your mind drifts off to other topics, there is no need to reprimand yourself. Simply think, "I don't want to think about this. I want to go back to my breathing." Even if you have to go back and forth dozens of times, you are doing mindfulness meditation correctly.

The trick is to notice the thoughts that inevitably occur to you when you focus on your breathing, rather than making them the primary focus. If you do this method of meditation every day, you will slowly get better at it. In time, you will find yourself truly mastering the technique of mindfulness meditation — focusing on your breath and nothing else.

Chapter 6: What Google Doesn't Tell You About Memory

A Practical Guide to the Processes of Memory

There are three processes that memories go through: encoding, storage, and retrieval. If you observe yourself carefully, you can see these processes in your brain in real time.

Let's use celebrity names as an example. The name of the hip hop artist Cardi B has probably made its way into your consciousness at some point, whether you are a fan or you barely know who she is.

The more times you heard her name, the more her name was pushed into your memory storage. On a cellular level, the synaptic connections that fired in response to hearing "Cardi B" fired enough to become a strong connection. When someone asks you to name a modern hip hop artist, you are able to say her name because "Cardi B" was a fairly strong connection. You can apply these three processes of memory to anything you want to remember or learn.

Knowing the processes that create memories will help you remember pieces of information like names and numbers. There are several learning techniques that will help you do this.

Before we get into techniques for memorizing pieces of information, you might have to readjust the way you think about memory. You might think that you are just "bad at remembering names."

People say this all the time: "I never forget a face, but I'm bad with names." This approach won't get you anywhere because it is defeatist. If you think you are just bad at remembering names, you won't learn names. Period. Get past that limiting approach and start being intentional with your memorization.

If you have a roster of students' names to memorize, you can't expect to learn them without devoting time to only learning their names. Put the roster to your left. To your right, copy down their names on notebook paper. It isn't as hard as you think it is. You will probably get them after looking at their faces and writing down their names just three of four times.

You have likely heard of pneumonic devices before. These are an excellent way to remember names.

The thing that keeps a lot of people from using pneumonic device is they are afraid that they are too embarrassing to use. They don't want people to find out about their pneumonic devices.

But if they are really so embarrassing, it doesn't even matter, because you will only keep them in your own head. There is no need to worry about someone finding out. People don't just randomly blurt out random private thoughts like odd pneumonic devices.

Take the names of co-workers, for example. Let's say you meet someone named Robert. You are trying to be more intentional with memorizing names, so you think to yourself: "He acts sort of robotic sometimes, so that will help me remember his name." Or maybe you know someone named David, and you remember his name by the Bible story of David and Goliath. You can remember his name because he is like the smaller David in the story. These are the kinds of ways you can remember names that are actually going to help you remember.

You can't feel ashamed of your deliberate attempts to remember things. No one truly learns anything without trying at all. Sure, sometimes we do remember things without giving it much effort, but that's not something you can expect most of the time. Usually, you will have to do some work to make the memorization happen.

Now, let's talk about numbers. For all numbers, be they phone numbers, zip codes, addresses, or anything else, the best method for remembering them is called chunking. You divide the numbers into different "chunks," because a group of small chunks is easier to remember than one long string of digits.

Take the number: 531924

This might look like it takes a good amount of work to memorize at first but look at it again. The last three numbers look like a year: 1924. Then the number before it is 53. The sequence 53, 1924 is a lot easier to remember than purely 531924. This is what chunking is. We can use chunking with a few more numbers where you might have to be more creative about how you use it.

3506227

Let's say this one is just a phone number. Phone numbers have some amount of chunking already built into them: it is 350-6227. You probably think of numbers like this already. You don't really memorize the whole thing, you just look at the first three numbers and then the next four numbers. You don't really think of the seven numbers altogether, even if you have it memorized.

Whether you use chunking or some other method, the most important thing you have to do is look for patterns in the numbers you try to memorize. In that last number, there were two 2's in a row. That would surely be easier to memorize than if they were two different numbers.

You can also use numbers that look like ages within your chunks to help you out. Maybe you will memorize the first three numbers as just 350, but then the next two as the ages 62 and 27.

You should try to make personal connections with numbers if it isn't obvious how you can chunk them out already. Look at another number: 9635835

While it is a little bit subjective, this number looks a little bit harder for me. It has two 35's, but the numbers around them don't follow much of a pattern. Separate out the 35's from the rest: 96, 35, 8, 35.

This means that you need to think of a way to remember 96 and 8. If you are a math whiz, you might think about what multiples or denominators the numbers share. The multiples method works perfectly here because 96 is a multiple of 8:

8*12=96

This is not to say that using math will be helpful to everyone. However, knowing about the relationships between numbers will help you a lot with memorizing them for situations like this. For this reason, I highly recommend you try to hone your mathematical intelligence. Look at the original number again: 9635835

Without chunking the number into 96, 35, 8, 35, it looks like another random hard-to-remember number. Chunking takes a little bit of practice, but if you try to learn to find some interest in math and be creative with the pneumonic devices you use for the items you memorize, it goes a very long way to remembering things.

There are other kinds of numbers you might want to learn, too. What if you hear a number spoken, and don't have it written anywhere that you can reference? These are the kinds of situations that really make people stressed about memorizing things.

Let's say you're on a road trip and someone tells you an address. You hear the address one time: 26603 Columbia Rd.

Read that address aloud once. Look away from the page for a moment and try to say it from memory.

I suspect that you found you were able to repeat it pretty easily. Why is that?

Saying things out loud is ultimately the best way you can get yourself to remember it. It is because it activates the most connections in our brain, giving our neurons more connections to refer to when we try to recall information.

When you say something out loud, your mouth makes a kind of muscle memory for what it is like to make the sound with your body. You think about the piece of information as a bit of language, so you also are thinking verbal-linguistically. When you spoke it, you also heard it again from yourself.

This goes for memorization, but also anything you want to learn, including deeper subjects: the more ways you use your brain to think about it, the easier you will learn it. Saying numbers out loud, even if we are looking at the number while we say it, is using your brain in all these different ways. Because of this, it is a really good way to memorize the number.

Go ahead and apply this to something more complex than memorization. Let's say you are dealing with a difficult problem at work. Your co-worker wants to increase the company budget, but your boss always says they don't want to increase the budget ever. When thinking through a difficult problem, talk about it aloud to yourself. Write down your thoughts in a private notebook that no one else will ever see. Type your thoughts into the Notes app on your phone. These are all different ways you can get your brain to process the issue, and I'm sure you could think of more.

Just like with methods to memorize names and numbers, we stop ourselves from using brain techniques that would help us, partially because we are embarrassed. There is no need to be embarrassed about trying to learn something, though. To begin with, if you are an adult who is really still afraid of being caught "trying," then maybe you should evaluate how you expect to improve yourself.

You should look at these memorization exercises as ways you can train your brain in general. Not only are you training your memory, but you are training yourself to be okay with being seen as someone who wants to improve themselves.

This a great way for people to see you — everyone could better themselves, and the fact that you are open about wanting to do more makes you more likable. Plus, now that you know new methods of learning people's names, they will like you more for calling them by name, too.

Chapter 7: All You Need Is Self-Discipline

A Realistic Approach to Learning Self-Discipline

If you take the words in this book to heart, you surely realized how hard it can be to put them into practice. And it's not all your fault.

You would expect that a chapter about self-discipline would tell you to accept all the blame for your actions and force yourself to change. But telling you that wouldn't help you.

Don't misunderstand me: it is kind of your fault. If it weren't, you wouldn't be able to change it. It's good that it's kind of your fault because that means you can take credit for taking control of yourself. But you can't change yourself through sheer force. If it were as easy as screaming at yourself in the mirror, "JUST DO IT!" like Shia LaBeouf, you would have done it already.

Your level of self-discipline is no more than all of your habits combined. Since you create your own habits, you can improve your self-discipline, but it isn't as simple as telling yourself to change. It isn't as simple as listening to a motivational speaker tell you how to change your life. Becoming an exemplar of self-discipline requires that you tackle one of your bad habits at a time.

As the waves hit the sandy shores of the beach, the shape of the shore slowly changes. Similarly, your brain slowly changes its texture depending on its inputs. It can change into what your environmental influences change it to be, or you can take command of your brain and lead the direction of your brain development.

Maybe you're sick of my philosophical ideas, but you have to think about the big questions if you want to get smart. When you take command of your synapses, directing how your brain changes, you are taking the role of an environmental influence. You are taking the role of an input.

That might be confusing because your environment consists of things that are outside of you. You can make choices that change how much time you spend around toxic people, but these people are still environmental influences, not you. You can change how much physical clutter you have in your home, but you can't quite say that your possessions are you. So, what does it mean to say that you should act like another influence?

Think of it as a feedback loop. Your personality and traits formed out of your genes and influences, but then you (your brain) formed its own identity. You have (your brain has) your own ideas about what you should do from this point. That makes it the same as the rest of your influences. These influences may have caused your brain to be what it is today, but now your brain plays its own role in affecting the trajectory of your development.

By no means am I suggesting that you can unilaterally determine what your brain becomes. You must be aware, by now, that improving your brain is a matter of realistically balancing things you can change with things you can't change.

I am saying this: there were things that made life hard for you, but without downplaying these realities, you shouldn't make excuses. Be honest with yourself — I can't know who you are, and no one is watching you read this section, so you can allow yourself to be honest — you certainly couldn't control all the things that happened to you. What happened did hold you back from your full potential some of the time.

But here is the cold, hard truth that you need to face. While there were unavoidable setbacks that kept you down, there were also times when you could have risen to the occasion and bettered yourself, and you didn't take the opportunity.

There are a number of words for this. The word "laziness" oversimplifies it too much; "apathy" doesn't quite work either. You might have cared, just not enough. Not enough to do anything.

The most appropriate word is "inertia." If you know anything about physics, your brain is making all the right connections right now. In physics, the principle of inertia states that an object in space only moves when force is placed upon it. If no force is placed upon an object, the object will not move.

I don't know what influences factored into your life. It might be that you had overbearing parents who were always placing force upon you to learn new skills and excel in school. It might be the opposite — no one expected you to do anything.

But inertia doesn't care what kind of background you have. For everyone, it works the same way. We, humans, are creatures of comfort. Generally speaking, if we are not required to do something, we will not do it. In other words, as a rule, we tend to only do exactly what is required of us, and nothing more.

It is undeniable that you missed opportunities in your life already, and that is a hard fact to face. Life is filled with opportunities, though. Now that you can see the role that inertia has played in your life, you can remember to use yourself as the environmental influence that pushes you to take the next opportunity. If no one else is there to push you, that force will have to come from you.

Through reading, you should have a better relationship with your brain than before. This will make being a positive influence on your brain easier for you. When you know how to meditate, it is easier to read your own thoughts and predict your future actions. It makes it easier to change the future path of your choices, too.

Meditation is only one of the things you have learned to do in this book, but you need to be aware of how truly important it is.

If you don't force yourself to meditate for at least ten minutes every day, you are not going to improve your brain in general. You might get better in some areas, but your overall awareness of your brain will stay the same. You can't expect to improve your brain if you are only working on skills that happen outside of your brain.

Maybe you still aren't convinced of the necessity of meditation, so we will cover some of the real benefits it has. Research has already been done on people who meditate to show the benefits they get from it. For one thing, in people who meditate, the part of the brain that is associated with the self is highly connected to the other parts.

This is only logical. It also shouldn't surprise you that the amount of gray matter in people who meditate is also higher. How much gray matter a person has is generally agreed upon to be a good indicator of someone's intelligence.

You probably didn't even need to learn these facts about the research on meditation, though. It is really quite intuitive why meditation gives a person benefit. The reason people don't meditate is they are afraid of what will happen if they let themselves be alone with their thoughts. Many people seem to go to bed with the TV on these days, so they don't even have to spend time with their thoughts before they go to sleep.

But this isn't a healthy way to live. If you have no relationship with your brain whatsoever, there is no way you can expect to train it to do more.

The benefits of meditation are good for anyone, but they are essential for you, someone who wants to achieve a lot. You are not content with a life that is just good enough; you want to chase your goals, and you know that achieving your goals will require you to attain more brainpower.

I can't overstate how much this ambition makes you unique. You may have noticed that most people are happy as long as they have the simple things in life. You should be happy with the simple things in life, too — that was what the minimalism chapter was all about. But you also learned how to be a minimalist so you could clear out the distractions that keep you from achieving your goals.

As you slowly become a person who meditates, your role as another environmental influence will become easier to fill. You will be able to jump between being inside your head and being outside of it, judging it from the outside.

When you are on the outside, you will have the ability to push your brain to be more than it already is. When you are on the inside, you can observe the truth of your current mental situation. It is necessary for you to be on both sides of your brain if you intend to learn self-discipline.

Learning self-discipline requires you to follow all the same guiding principles that we have covered so far. If you want to improve your memory, you will have the practice the learning techniques from the memory chapter. It will take time and patience. Anyone who is required to do what is necessary in the moment will push their brains to adapt. It is often difficult and uncomfortable, but the benefits that you reap afterwards are absolutely worth it.

One great example is the famous study of cab drivers in London. London is a complex network of streets, so these drivers had to adapt to this. They had to push their brains to do more than they were probably comfortable with because they had no choice. Cab drivers are working people, and if they didn't adapt to driving on these roads, they wouldn't be able to make money.

In the study, the brains of these drivers were scanned. What was found was astounding — one part of the brains of these drivers was uncommonly large. You can guess what function this brain part is needed for memory. The hippocampus of cab drivers in London were found to be extremely large, meaning that their memories literally and physically improved out of necessity.

I said that you had to become your own environmental influence and push your brain to do more. In the case of the London cab drivers, they absolutely had to do this, because they had no choice. It was either they learned how to navigate London, or they weren't able to earn enough money to live. But your situation might not be as dire as that.

We usually find a way to deal with situations when we have no other choice but to confront them. What is harder is when a situation is not life or death, but we are not content with things staying as they are. There is not a strict day of the year when we have to finish our goals, so we keep pushing away our goals to the next month, and then the next month. We don't ever feel the urgency of doing the work required to achieve our goals today, because there is always the next month.

It is vital that you are not discouraged by this. It's human nature, so it's completely natural. You are not fundamentally different from anyone who did achieve their goals, so you can find a way around this natural tendency just like they did.

What you have to make yourself do is see the urgency of your goals. You will become more disciplined when you truly grasp how limited your time is. There is no real deadline for your goal because you could live your entire life without achieving it. You have to make a deadline each month that addresses one small aspect of your goals at a time.

Tackling your goal one small task at a time keeps it manageable enough, so you don't keep pushing it away out of fear. Fear is, unfortunately, a big reason that people keep pushing their goals farther down in the calendar. They are secretly afraid that they are not actually capable, so they never start.

Even if you secretly believe that you are not capable enough, you will feel much more confident in the smaller steps that lead up to the larger goal. Let's say that your goal is to own a house. That might seem like too much to confront at once, and you don't even know where to begin. You might have a secret fear that you will never own a house because you never have before, and you can't imagine it being any other way. You might be afraid that there is a fundamental reason for this — that some people have natural self-discipline to work hard, and this is why they own their house. You might think that people who own their houses aren't like you, and they are more capable.

But you are completely capable, so you can banish those negative, self-sabotaging thoughts. I want you to confront the real issue instead of being distracted by your emotions. Even if you can't shake away the feeling that you aren't good enough, don't spend time trying to change your emotions. They don't matter. What matters is changing your situation — once you do that, there is no way you will believe that you aren't capable. You will see how unreasonable it was for you to think that you weren't capable.

Your goal isn't to own a house. Your goal is to open a savings account. Once you have a savings account, you will feel the need to be more careful with how you spend money, so you will start to accumulate some funds. That habit will keep you financially afloat, and your rent will always be paid on time.

A year will come that you have a great credit rating, and you will have the extra money to feel like a mortgage is a good investment. Then you can start looking at reasonably priced houses and sign your mortgage with the bank.

Notice how much more reasonable your goals sound when you break them down into smaller parts. This pathway towards owning a house doesn't sound like an impossible dream; it sounds like something that can really happen, given you have patience with yourself and let everything happen one step at a time.

It works the same way with any of your goals. Remember to keep chasing your dreams by taking the role of an environmental influence and pushing yourself. You can't let inertia run its course, or nothing will change in your life.

When you push yourself, it is not something that you can just do one day. Your goals come in many smaller steps, so you have to push yourself to do the small steps every day. But getting yourself to act is easier when you think about how small the steps really are. You aren't pushing yourself to do everything today. It is only one small step. That small step will be worth it if you do the next step on the following day.

It doesn't matter how small the steps are. What matters is that you take them every day. If you do them every day for a month, they will become habits, part of your network of synapses.

It will become part of your brain's design to stay on the trajectory to achieving your goals. When you get to that point, it will be so much easier.

Chapter 8: Declutter Your Body, Mind, Time and Environment

Finding Yourself in the Larger World

Have you heard the expression, "Look at who you are with, that is who you are"? You could also say, "Look at where you are; that is who you are." However, you would describe yourself or however others would describe you, you were not created in a vacuum.

Besides physical traits like height or eye color, there are very few traits that you were always destined to have. If you consider yourself quiet, there is a reason for that. Maybe you grew up in a calmer, less boisterous family. Maybe you looked up to fictional characters who fit into the strong, silent type.

But whatever personality you think you have now, it can change. The prefrontal cortex, the brain region right behind your forehead, created your personality based on the information you took in from your environment. Some of it, you decided to incorporate into your personality.

If you spend more time observing the thoughts going through your prefrontal cortex and reflecting on how your environment created these thoughts, you can make yourself whoever you want to be. Control your environment, the way you spend your time, and the people you spend time with, and you will control yourself.

It is no more complicated than that. Now, I want you to do some more meditation so you can reflect on what factors in your environment might be keeping you from reaching your full potential. You won't be able to reach your goals if you don't deal with these things, whatever they are.

The hardest ones will be the people in your life who hold you back. If there is one person or more who holds you back in life, you know who they are. You might not want to admit it to yourself, but in the back of your mind, you know who it is. Without that person in your life, you would get closer to success in mental mastery. Let's discuss some of the reasons for this.

First, there are the ones you might have already guessed. If you have friends who take you down the wrong path, they change the way you spend your time. Instead of working on that novel or planning that trip around the world, you waste your time with them, doing nothing that will help you in the long run.

This is not to say that spending time with your friends is bad. It is good — remember, social life is not a luxury as a human. It is a need. If our social needs aren't met, we suffer. The issue isn't about spending time with friends in general. It's spending time with people who keep you down.

There are a lot of ways someone could do this. Maybe you spend a lot of time with someone because you have a history with them, even though they treat you poorly. You don't know what your life would be like without them so it scares you to think about what life would be like without them, even though they make you feel down. This is an emotional way that someone can hold you back.

They could be holding you back financially. Does your significant other contribute to your life? If you have kids, do they help with them? If you don't have kids, do they have a job? Are you working on your finances as a team?

These are the logistical ways that someone can hold you back. But think back to the quote I gave you at the beginning of the chapter: "Look at who you are with, that is who you are." People can hold you back by wasting your time or directly pushing you in the wrong direction, but they don't have to be intentionally holding you back to be a detriment to your goals.

If you smoke, you're probably not the only person you know who smokes. I can basically guarantee you that your friends smoke if you smoke. You can apply this to any person; the reason it's true is because of how susceptible our brains are to influence. The connections in our brain are what give it structure. The things that cause these connections to form are our influences.

The brain is extremely manipulable, which is why you never have to give up hope that things can change for you. But the point I want to drive home is that you won't be able to make these changes until you change your surroundings. You may think that you are so determined that you can be different from everyone in your environment, and maybe they will change with you. But that is not how people work.

You became like the people around you because they influenced you. They changed the actual structure of your brain just by being around you.

If you want to be smart, you have to be around people who are smart. You don't get smart by seeming smart to your less smart friends. If anything, it holds you back to be around people who don't make you feel dumb sometimes. If you feel dumb sometimes around someone, it's because you're learning something from them. You're not learning things from people who don't contribute anything to your life.

By no means am I telling you to change your social environment entirely. I am not telling you to leave your whole life behind and never talk to your friends and family again. They can still be a part of your life, even if you do think they hold you back sometimes. That is life, after all. You can't just run away from people.

But you can add new influences to your life to be alongside your old ones. These new stimuli will change you because they are a new model for how to be a person. Without models, we can't learn anything.

The reason that our influences are so influential is truly fascinating. We have a specialized type of neuron in our brains called mirror neurons.

Mirror neurons are a very exciting new thing that brain researchers have been learning a lot about in the last few years. In one study, scientists scanned the brain of a monkey as it watched another monkey hold a banana. At the same time, they scanned the brain of the monkey holding the banana.

When the researchers looked at the brain scans, they found that both monkeys had specialized neurons activating at the time that the banana was being held. The monkey holding the banana fired this neuron at the same time that the monkey watching them fired it.

This specialized neuron was a mirror neuron. We, humans, have mirror neurons, too. They apply to everything we do that involves empathy. If we can imagine someone doing something, we can fire a mirror neuron that replicates them doing it. When a person actually does that thing, the same mirror neuron fires.

This discovery is amazing because it means in a lot of ways, thinking about doing something is the same thing as doing it, at least from the perspective of your brain. You might say that it makes sense, though. As you read this book about the brain and all sorts of applications it has in your life, you aren't literally looking into your skull and looking at the parts of your brain.

But with the power of words and mirror neurons, you pretty much were able to do that, just now. You are not limited to what you can actually physically do. Thanks to mirror neurons, you are only limited by your imagination.

You'll want to think about the conversations that you have with your friends and consider whether they spark your imagination, or just keep you stagnant. If it's the latter, then you'll never change as long as they never change.

We have covered the fact that you have to take control of the environment you live in, including the people you surround yourself with. But this isn't the only clutter that you have to take care of. If you want to improve your brainpower, you have to declutter your mind. We will go over some straightforward ways to do this.

Even after reading the third chapter about the biology of the brain, you might still see the brain as something mysterious that you can't really understand. In a way, since there are still things about it we don't understand, we are allowed to feel a little bit mystified by the brain. There is nothing wrong with that. But even while you maintain that the brain is sort of mysterious, you have to ask yourself some questions about what your brain is. You have to ask yourself what thoughts are. These are philosophical questions that have been asked for ages. In more recent years, scientific advances have found some answers to what thoughts are.

The psychologist Edward Tolman did a famous experiment with mice. You have probably seen versions of this experiment in popular media: Tolman put the mice in a maze and tried to see if they could find a way out. He didn't give him a trail of food to follow or give them any guide whatsoever. These mice were truly stuck in a maze, and the only way they could escape was by trying different routes until they found the right one.

The results were ground-breaking in the study of mammal's brains. The mice were able to get out of Tolman's maze. (Even as a human, the idea of having to find my way out of a maze sounds very stressful and difficult!)

The conclusion that Tolman and his colleagues came to realize was that mice must have mental maps in their brains that allowed them to think through the maze. The mice were not limited to thinking about what was in front of them; they could "see" the maze they were trapped inside in their little mouse brains. Their mental maps allowed them to escape and were ultimately instrumental in getting them out.

Mice don't have nearly as many synapses as we do, but they were still able to complete this complicated task. The experiment answered Tolman's question about whether we store mental maps in our brains, but some of the philosophical questions we have been asking for centuries are still making our heads hurt today.

What are thoughts, really? Are they words? Are they sound in our heads? We know that our brains are ultimately collections of synapses on the microscopic level, but how do synapses translate to thoughts?

Other experiments sought to answer these same questions. In one, they artificially caused a synapse to fire in mice multiple times in one second or just one time in one second. In the mice whose synapses were stimulated a lot, the scientists could see in their brains that they got to keep the connection. When the synapse was artificially stimulated only once, the synapse actually faded away.

This experiment seems to confirm what we have already said in the book so far. When we use our synapses, we keep them. If we stop using them, they go away.

In this way, the way synapses work is no different from how we know memories to work. If we stop thinking about certain memories, we will eventually forget them, because our brains stopped "practicing" firing those synapses. If we think about a memory a lot, it's not likely to go anywhere anytime soon.

Alas, much research has been done on these questions, but it's hard to know if we'll ever be getting real answers. It's possible that we're asking the wrong questions, too. After all, when we ask where thoughts begin, it's sort of like asking where the sea begins. Does the sea begin in Florida or China? The Arctic or the Pacific?

Since our brains are the home of so much rich activity, mapping out one thought would likely be the equivalent of writing a whole book of binary code. It would be impossible to read, and impossible to understand. We can understand some things about thoughts, so not all hope is lost. But as humans, we are not yet at a point where we can answer these questions with as much specificity as we might like.

Just think about how much is happening in your brain right now. Your eyes are scanning this text, and you have built-in connections about these words that you can use to interpret them. All of this is happening quickly and seamlessly. You aren't even consciously aware of most of what is happening; it is so ingrained in your mind that you don't have to think through each word.

One study at UC Berkley asked participants to name an antonym for the word "humid." At the same time, the participants' brains were scanned for electrical activity. It was a marvelous sight to behold for the scientists: when the participants were first asked to name an antonym, in less than a second, there was electrical activity further back in the brain. This means their unconscious brains were working on answering the question before their conscious brains came in. After the electrical activity in the back was finished, it faded away, and there was electrical activity in the front. The front is where your prefrontal cortex and frontal lobe are, which are in control of your conscious thought.

This study tells us that our brains do a lot of the work they do automatically; we don't have to monitor them to push them to do their job. If we have had exposure to something or practice with it, that thing is simply a part of us, and we can rely on it later. The frontal lobe only came in at the very end when the participants gave the scientists their final answer.

Another thing to note about this study was the wide range of areas that lit up with electricity. Even for something as simple as finding an antonym for a word, a great number of regions were recruited by the brain.

We can assume that not every area that lit up with electricity was needed, but that the question simply made the participant think about things that were semi-related but irrelevant to answering the question (not all on a conscious level, of course). If that weren't the case, it wouldn't make sense that we would need so much cranial real estate just for one word.

I hope learning about these experiments gave you some insight into what your brain really is and how it works. Knowing how your brain works should give you some insight about how to declutter it.

We learned that a lot of your unconscious brain is lit up just for finding an antonym for this word: long.

When you came up with "short," multiple areas in the back of your brain just lit up, areas that you don't have direct control over, because they are unconscious. This fact teaches us an important lesson in clearing our minds: decluttering our minds doesn't mean making them stop running.

Our brains are always running, even when we are asleep. In particular, the parts of our brains that are unconscious never stop going. And these parts make up the bulk of your brain.

That means if your goal is to clear your mind of clutter, it is pointless to make your goal "stop having unrelated thoughts." Unrelated thoughts will run through your mind constantly because of your unconscious brain. You can't stop them, and you don't want to, because they are keeping your synapses engaged.

Instead, your goal should be to know what your conscious brain wants, as a separate entity from your unconscious brain. "My unconscious brain keeps bringing up unpleasant thoughts about that social interaction I had the other day, but I have no control over that. Instead, I'll focus on keeping my conscious brain thinking about the new leads I'm going to call for my business tomorrow."

This is a good lesson for your brain in general. Since there are so many connections in it, you can't expect to micromanage and control each of them. Instead, you should focus on keeping your conscious mind coming back to your goal for the day.

It's exactly like coming back to the breath in mindfulness meditation, so continuing to practice mindfulness will help you declutter your mind as well. Don't waste your time stressing over micromanaging all the ideas and thoughts that flood through your mind when you meditate and don't waste your time with that throughout the day, either.

Accept the fact that they will sometimes distract you and get you off track, and make your goal simply returning to your conscious mind's focus.

Chapter 9: How To Hijack Your Circumstances

Keeping Track of Your Habits to Change Them

When you think of mindfulness, you probably think of sitting cross-legged somewhere in the mountains of Tibet, humming "OM." This is one part of mindfulness, but it is just one.

A person who spends all their time on the reflective aspect is not practicing mindfulness. Find a place where you can make notes, even if it's an app on your phone. Write today's date and the date will be one month from now. Set a recurring reminder on your phone during a time that you are not busy.

When you get this reminder, don't meditate, but take a few minutes to think about what you did that day. Don't overthink it. If you went shopping, vacuumed, and sorted through bills, listing all those things is all you need to do.

It doesn't seem like much, but if you do this every day, you will become more aware of what your life consists of.

When the month ends, think of one thing you want to change about your life. Think of one small thing you can do every day to make it happen.

Recall from Chapter 8 that you have to change your environment to change your brain. Your brain has become what it is today because of the stimuli you have had in your environment. This chapter is about the practical ways you can go about making these changes.

But while that chapter was mostly focused on changing the people in your life, this one is about your habits and how they made your brain, yourself.

I've said repeatedly in this book that your brain changes depending on the inputs you give it. We've gone over multiple examples of how we know this to be the case.

If you introduce a new habit into your routine, the habit will change you over time. You just have to be patient. Slowly, you will notice a lot of things that you thought were set in stone about yourself are like putty — you can mold them however you please.

There are so many different goals that you could have in mind with wanting to change your habits and change your brain. I couldn't possibly cover all of them, but we will use the nine intelligences as a framework for different goals you might have.

Becoming a master of your own brain takes a healthy amount of self-awareness, too. If you can't be honest with yourself about where your talents currently are, you won't be able to improve. If you aren't able to repeat a pitch, lying to yourself about what you are currently able to do is not going to help you get better. On the contrary, you have to think about what you still don't know how to do.

Take musical-rhythmic intelligence as an example. You might not be able to repeat a pitch or keep a beat, and you shouldn't just assume that you can. You have to actually test these things out for yourself.

Ask a friend who is already musically inclined to test it out for you. Are you able to repeat back the same pitch as they give you?

Don't be discouraged if you can't do it. All that it means is you have some practicing to do. If you keep at it and don't give up, you'll be able to pick up this skill just as you picked up any skill.

Your friends can help you out a lot with musical-rhythmic intelligence if they know how to play music, but maybe they don't. What do you do then?

We live in the age of information, so what you have to do is use the Internet. Try to find books about music that interest you. You might want to make connections to talents that you already have. There are books about the relation between music and math; there are books about the relation between music and words.

You can find a book about any topic these days. You can also do research about how you can learn about whatever you want online. There are video tutorials and websites dedicated to the intelligence you want to work on.

Don't get discouraged when you don't pick up something right away. It's like everything we have gone over so far: it's not the speed with which you pick things up that counts, it's your consistency with coming back to it. The way you keep a consistent pace with honing an intelligence is by making it a part of your daily routine.

Choose a time of day that you try to be more musical. You can spend this time in a variety of different ways, as long as it relates to music somehow. You can read a book about it or do research online about it.

It works exactly the same way with any intelligence you want to learn. You have to make sure it pushes the limits of what you are comfortable with. If you take verbal-linguistic intelligence as an example, you can't expect to become a master of language through reading alone. You have to write, too. And don't forget to work on your speaking and listening skills. Each of these embodies an important part of verbal-linguistic intelligence, and none are more important than the other.

With any new habit that you track, you have to think as small as possible. Your goal can't be "get better at speaking." You have to make a small, actionable goal that connects directly to that larger goal. Instead, make your goal, "Join a speech class." Once you join a class, make a new small goal. "Give a whole speech without saying any filler words." And so on.

This applies to any intelligence that you work on. You can't make your goal for logical-mathematical intelligence, "Get better at doing mental math." It's not specific enough, so you'll never get started on it. Make your goal, "Spend 30 minutes every night working on math problems."

To reiterate, if you want to change your circumstances, you have to change your habits one at a time. This will happen in two basic steps. First, go through your regular routine for a month and keep track of what you do every day. The second step is to replace one of the things you do as part of your routine with something that will help you change.

This way, you are not really making yourself do anything extreme. You will be doing all the same things as before, but instead of doing X, you will fill that same slot of time by doing Y.

Stop making a routine of watching reruns every night. Instead, fill in that slot of time with learning about a new diet you can go on. Fill in that slot with some simple cardio exercises. Even going on a walk for ten minutes will help you improve your bodily-kinesthetic intelligence. It might not seem like much, but over time, these small changes in your behavior add up, and they make you a new person.

Rewiring your brain is only a matter of changing your behavior. It can be hard to get started, but once you do, it isn't nearly as bad as you imagined it being. Starting is the hardest part because it requires you to challenge the connections that you have already built in your brain. At the moment, it is so much easier on our brains to keep going with the habits we already have set.

In the long run, you will be glad that you stretched outside of your comfort zone. You will feel more fulfilled as a person because you will have realized all the things you were capable of but didn't think to push yourself to do before.

You will have to think for yourself what you have to do to some extent, but I will give you some ideas for each of the intelligences. Let's take visual-spatial intelligence as an example.

Everyone had to take an art class at some point, so you must have learned some skills in drawing, even if you were never the best. Think of the last art class you took and what artistic skill you learned. Try to do what you learned in class now as an adult. Do you see what you could improve on?

Sometimes, it can be very daunting to start working on a new intelligence because we have no idea where to start. Starting is hard enough because our brains are used to following certain patterns without diverging from them. But starting a new intelligence is also hard because there are so many places where we could start, and we don't know which one to choose.

The choice can feel arbitrary. If you want to work on visual-spatial skills, do you take an art class? Do you spend more time with your artistic friends and ask them to help you? We always think that we want more choices, but truth be told, having more choices can make us stay still, preventing us from doing anything at all.

The important thing is not what you do, but that you do it. It doesn't matter what you pick, as long as you pick something that has to do with the intelligence. It's never going to be perfect anyway. Doing it at all is what you want to focus on.

Interpersonal and intrapersonal intelligences can be a little more straightforward for how you approach them. You will learn a lot of skills that can apply to the other intelligences.

You might see intrapersonal intelligence as an introvert's intelligence, but that isn't always necessarily the case. People can love being around others and still have a strong connection to themselves. Maybe you consider yourself to be like this. You are a reader, but you also like to be with friends and meet new people.

Neither one is more important than the other. In fact, if you want to know yourself, you will want to be around other people. As we discussed in the chapter about decluttering your life, the people you surround yourself with are very influential in the person you become.

On the other hand, if you want to have good social skills, being aware of yourself is important, too. Other people are much more like us than we think. There are times when well-meaning individuals will harm their relationships with others not because they are thoughtless, but because they don't put themselves in others' shoes.

You might have a good idea of how to be friendly with people you know, but are absolutely clueless about how to interact with strangers. This is a situation where a balance between intrapersonal and interpersonal intelligence really comes in handy.

The longer you spend with yourself doing mindfulness meditation, the more you realize the effect others have on you. Their words reverberate across your mind, eventually becoming your own. We don't even realize that we are using someone else's ideas a lot of the time, because once we hear some idea, it just becomes part of us. We come to believe it, and that idea becomes ours.

Existential-moral intelligence might be the most intimidating for a lot of people. Not everyone wants to think deeply all of the time, which is understandable. They might have a lot going on in their lives already that makes them want to avoid filling them with more stresses about the wider context.

In honing your existential-moral intelligence, you don't have to become a totally new person. You don't have to change everything that you believe about yourself and the world. If you want to improve your brain, though, you do want to keep the big questions in your mind from time to time.

You might think that philosophers are only ever asking questions that can never be answered. But the point of asking questions is not always to get answers. If you want to become smarter, you have to learn the value of questions themselves. Even if we never get to the bottom of a philosophical issue, there is still much value to getting ourselves to think about it.

In the modern age, it can be especially common for us to feel disconnected from the natural world. We are so accustomed to our mass-produced, automated world that nature can feel like something in the background that doesn't require much attention.

But I hope that this book itself has made you question that idea to some extent. You came from nature yourself, after all. Finding your place in it is sure to make you smarter, and happier, too. Like with the others, you don't have to change everything about your life to be more naturalistically-minded. Just add a few things into your life that keep you connected to nature.

Keep some plants in your house and water them. Grow something in your yard besides grass. Have animals in your life besides cats and dogs.

Do you have any family who lives in the country? You should visit them. These days, most of us live in cities, but there are also people living in the country who might be able to help you reconnect with the natural world. They can give you a tour of the nature in the area. Ask about what kinds of plants grow there. Ask what animals live there. You should learn the answers to these questions in your own neighborhood.

I am giving you so many possibilities in this chapter to get your imagination going. You sculpt your brain through your actions. If you were already someone who took care of plants, you would think of yourself as that kind of person.

You can still be that person now, but you have to stop thinking that what you are now is permanent. You are changing constantly no matter what, so you might as well take some control over the direction you go in.

This applies most clearly to your emotions. You have probably been there before. You were extremely anxious, and the emotions that were running through you were so strong, that it seemed like it was going to last forever; maybe you were terribly depressed for weeks, and it seemed like this was your only option. Much like your emotions, your habits can seem like they are the only way you can be when you live them out.

Even though humans have evolved to be extremely smart, our intelligence is sometimes overshadowed by short-sightedness. In babies, there is a stage of development called object permanence. Before this stage, if a baby doesn't see a ball in front of them, they completely forget that it exists. But as the baby matures, they come to learn that the ball continues existing even when they aren't looking at it.

Of course, you know now that things continue to exist when you don't see them. But you still have a cognitive bias that makes you believe that your present defines your future. It isn't easy for you to see how things could be different.

It might seem like we are overusing the word "imagination," but the word is so important to everything in this book. If you didn't have an imagination, you wouldn't ever change. That's because we have to envision what the change will look like before we get there. We have to know where we want to go before we go there.

When you were depressed and doing nothing but lying on the couch, scrolling mindlessly through social media, you couldn't imagine how things could be good. You felt like you would never be happy again. Then time passed, and you were happy again. That doesn't mean that you were always happy on your way there, but change did occur.

Life is constantly changing. It's one thing we can always count on — so if you think that changing your habits and becoming intelligent in a new area is impossible for you, you are flat-out wrong. You already changed immensely from whoever you were in the past. When you inevitably change in the future, it will be due to the small things that happen every day. One day at a time, you will become a new person.

You are going to change in the future anyway, so you might as well plan for some of the things that change about you. There isn't a way you can control every single thing in your daily life, so you can't micromanage every part of you that changes. But you can imagine a few directions you would like to go, name them, and find the practical ways you can get there in your everyday life.

The only way you can train your brain to be greater is little by little. The only way you can make yourself change is one day at a time.

Conclusion

Thank you for making it through to the end of Rewire Your Brain, let's hope it was informative and able to provide you with all of the tools you need to achieve your goals whatever they may be.

Only you can see what happens in your own mind, so only you can confront your habits and change them. You can study yourself from the inside and create yourself anew. Your thoughts and behaviors are one. You must resist your bad habits and commit to new actions to form new habits.

Take control of your environment and the people you surround yourself with. This will make becoming a better you possible.

It is also essential that you adopt a minimalist mindset, removing the obstacles and distractions that hinder you. Minimize all things but your priorities. These are your physical needs as an animal and your human needs: socialization and self-efficacy. Achieving self-efficacy is as simple as making your talent a part of your everyday routine.

The next step is to stop living with your old habits. You know the secret to sculpting a brain of your own design. It's time to form new habits that make a new you and leave behind the person you were before.

You have everything you need in the fresh synaptic connections you made by reading this book. If you notice any of them starting to prune, revisit the corresponding chapters until the information moves into your long-term memory.

Since your memories become more durable the more times you reinforce them, we will conclude by reviewing what we have learned. Your brain picks up on your behaviors and turns them into habits, inclining you to continue doing them in the future. At first, it won't feel natural to act outside of your habits. But you'll get over the initial discomfort, and you'll be glad you challenged your bad habits with new behaviors.

Improving your brain only takes changing some of your bad habits. If you follow the guidance in this book, nothing will stop you from reaching your potential. And your potential is limitless.

www.ingramcontent.com/pod-product-compliance
Lightning Source LLC
Chambersburg PA
CBHW071420210526
45465CB00001B/465